A Catholic University

A Catholic University
Vision and Opportunities

Terrence J. Murphy

A Michael Glazier Book

THE LITURGICAL PRESS
Collegeville, Minnesota

www.litpress.org

A Michael Glazier Book published by The Liturgical Press.

Cover design by Greg Becker.

1   2   3   4   5   6   7   8   9

ISBN 0-8146-5101-1 (softcover)
ISBN 0-8146-5118-6 (casebound)

Contents

Preface

Colleges and universities are intimately related to the development of people and the well-being of society. Their rich diversity in the United States offers a great variety of opportunities for people to develop their talents and enhance society. They are the wellspring of democratic government, as well as a prosperous economy, both of which require the ability, skill, and intelligent leadership of educated people. While there is great diversity among institutions of higher education, they have many common purposes and shared activities; hence, the experience of one university may be of benefit to others. And so, it is my hope that the experience of the University of St. Thomas may be helpful to other colleges and universities.

The question is often asked: Why did St. Thomas grow so much during a very difficult time in American society and in higher education, the turbulent era of the civil rights movement, Vietnam War, student protests, and Second Vatican Council? This book is an attempt to answer that question, among others. The first part deals largely with the university's mission, its commitment to moral and religious principles; the second treats of the application of these principles in service to the community in an entrepreneurial environment. St. Thomas held to its basic religious and educational commitments which accentuated the desire to serve a broader community and an entrepreneurial spirit. In describing what went on, I had to eliminate or save for another occasion many informative insights and incidents. This is not a history of the University of St. Thomas during the twenty-five years of one presidency. Nor is it a suggestion that the path of St. Thomas should be followed by others: one size does not fit all. However, there are advantages to institutions sharing their best practices, their vision, and their experiences. They learn from each other.

The general public may also find this book helpful because of the fundamental importance of higher education, and hopefully, members of the higher-education community will thoughtfully consider the positions advanced here. Students may find this account useful as they look for a college or university which fits their needs and goals. There is a vast array of material published each year that advertises the strength of various institutions, so much so that it can be a burden for them to analyze it when they are choosing a college. This account may help students and their parents to decide what are some characteristics of higher education important to them and thus enable them to choose those institutions that best suit them.

As one looks at the great strength and diversity of higher education, one's admiration grows. Our free and democratic institutions serve different segments of our population. They nourish our society and at the same time are strengthened by the freedom and vitality of that society.

The development of St. Thomas during the twenty-five years considered in this book was a group effort. No one person can claim credit for it. It represents the hard work, creativity, and commitment of many persons—so many that it would be presumptuous to try to mention even a representative sample of them. One person to whom I am especially indebted is my secretary for many years, Mrs. Kathleen Boyd. She has spent uncounted hours putting the manuscript on the computer, proofreading it, and attending to the many details necessary for publication. For her untiring efforts I am deeply grateful.

Terrence J. Murphy

I. Catholic Higher Education for a Fuller Life

1

Education, Religion, Leadership

If a university is to be truly universal, as its name implies, religion should have a place in its educational thrust. A secular university, whether public or private, belies its universal character if theology is missing in its course offerings. Religion can enrich the academic disciplines to which it is relevant. As it influences the education of young people, it can build better people and better communities and become an agent of change in the marketplace and the public forum. It can be an energizing factor, moving universities to greater service to their communities. Many private universities still hold to the tradition of relating education and religion in the interest of enriching academic disciplines and of enhancing life and society.

This necessarily raises questions about the vitality and depth of religious convictions and about the relevancy of religious principles and values to academic disciplines and to public life. Is religion a passive presence in the life of the university or is it in the forefront as a dynamic driving force? Is it relegated to the private lives of students and others, not regarded as a potent force for a better community and for the development of fuller lives for its adherents? If there is a place for religion in the marketplace and the public square, how does it get there?

The historical background for our present lack of religion in higher education is instructive. When Western civilization struggled to crawl out from under the cloud of devastation and ignorance left after the fall of the Roman Empire and the wreckage wrought by the invading barbarians, schools were established at monasteries and cathedrals. These schools grew into the great universities of Europe: the universities of

3

Paris, Bologna, Oxford, and Cambridge, among others. As they grew into independent institutions, they retained the religious dimension of their curricula.

The first great universities of the new world were part of that intellectual-religious tradition. Harvard University owes its foundation to religious-minded people who cherished both learning and religion and wanted them interrelated. Harvard set the pattern which spread across the United States.

However, the nineteenth century saw a turning away from religion and its values in education. The leaders of this revolution in education were not, for the most part, anti-religious. Some saw religion as irrelevant to learning, but for most, practical considerations moved them. The multitude of denominations and beliefs made it difficult—some would say impossible—to include religious considerations in universities open to people of all religious persuasions and to those of none at all.

The people who dominated higher education after the Civil War wanted to create a unified national culture. They wanted a culture so broadly and deeply accepted that another civil war would be unlikely. Religious divisions, they thought, would hinder such unity. Higher education could promote a national culture and unity. Hence, there could be no place for religion in public universities.

Moreover, the churches were not really challenging the academy to integrate religious values and concepts with new knowledge. They and the academy were not speaking to one another at a deeper intellectual level, although they maintained pleasant associations. As universities grew and welcomed people of all persuasions, denominations which sponsored a university often found it difficult or impossible to support the university, which then had to look to nonreligious sources for financial support. Thus, the churches' influence was further eroded. Religion was removed from the curriculum for several practical reasons and not because of any inherent conflict between religion and reason. Religion drifted to the margins of the campuses and their intellectual life. This separation continues and constitutes a major problem for universities and for our society. Religion is a major interest of the American people, as is education, yet each maintains a respectful distance from the other. As George Marsden has written: "Religion came to be regarded as essentially an extra-curricular activity."[1]

---

[1] George M. Marsden, *The Outrageous Idea of Christian Scholarship* (New York: Oxford University Press, 1997) 17.

James Burtchaell has written at length on the decline of religion in the Protestant church-related colleges. He summarizes his study as follows: "The elements of the slow but apparently irrevocable cleavage of colleges from churches were many. The church was replaced as a financial patron by alumni, foundations, philanthropists, and government. The regional accrediting associations, the alumni, and the government replaced the church as the primary authorities to whom the colleges would give an accounting of stewardship. The study of their faith became academically marginalized and the understanding of religion was degraded by translation into reductive banalities for promotional use. . . . The faculty transferred their primary loyalties from their college to their disciplines and their guilds, and were thereby antagonistic to any competing norms of professional excellence related to the church."[2] The long-term result, as Stephen Carter noted, is that "law and politics have trivialized religion in the public square."[3] Burtchaell sees some Catholic colleges and universities already on the same slippery slope that Protestant universities followed into a secular existence. Will Catholic institutions eventually lose their Catholic identity and become secular?

While religious principles find little place in public classrooms, some private church-related colleges and universities have continued, with varying degrees of success, to relate religious and moral values to academic disciplines. This book is about one such effort and pertains only to certain aspects of that effort which endeavors to reclaim for religion the ground it lost. It looks to the early European traditions of education and religion and attempts to embody their values and lessons in contemporary higher education.

If value-oriented education is to play a larger role in the academy and the community, new leadership is required—entrepreneurial leadership. Universities are complex organizations that call for a wide range of talents on the part of their leaders, especially their chief executives. Among such talents are creativity, convictions, industriousness, and especially the willingness to take risks. Educational leadership is an important topic in this book.

Much will be written about entrepreneurial leadership. Entrepreneurship is not a common characteristic of educational leadership, yet

[2] James Tunstead Burtchaell, *The Dying of the Light* (Grand Rapids, Mich.: Eerdmans, 1998) 837.

[3] Stephen L. Carter, *The Culture of Disbelief: How American Law and Politics Trivialize Religious Devotion* (New York: Basic Books, 1993).

it can be a distinctive characteristic of a university and raise the university to new levels of excellence and service. When it embraces religion, it can create a whole new dimension that moves the university beyond the campus and enriches society. This book will deal with these two topics throughout, namely, entrepreneurial leadership and religion, especially Catholicism, that reach out to individuals and society.

Leadership embraces not just the president but also the trustees, administrators, faculty, students, and alumni. This leadership, in all its segments, must be enlightened, entrepreneurial, risk-taking, and open to new opportunities, but more importantly, it must be faith-filled and grounded in the fundamental role of religious and moral values in higher education.

Evidence of this will be seen in the growth and development of the university described in this book. The pages that follow discuss each of the elements of this vision of private higher education, positioning the discussion on a real-life campus during a quarter century. It describes how, under entrepreneurial leadership and with the conviction of the worth of its value-oriented education for the betterment of the community, one small, Midwestern liberal arts college tried to live out its commitment to moral and religious values and to the community's well-being. In the process, growing in size and academic stature, it became a successful, comprehensive university—the University of St. Thomas in St. Paul, Minnesota.

2

The Religious Mission of a Catholic University

During a quarter century, St. Thomas, which became a university in 1990, grew fivefold and developed from a college into a successful comprehensive university. So dramatic was the change that observers, at home and abroad, asked, How did this happen? Were the changes intentional and planned? Who was responsible? What enables an institution of higher learning to undertake new and quality programs in areas crucial to the health of a community, in education, business, management, law, ministry, communications, international studies, counseling, social work, computer software, and engineering, and at the same time broaden and deepen its religious commitment?

A survey of public awareness of St. Thomas in the late 1970s indicated it was not well known, even in the state of Minnesota. A typical statement was, "I have the impression it is well regarded, but I don't know much about it." It grew from a small liberal arts college of local influence to a medium-size teaching university with a strong liberal arts component and vital religious/ethical commitments. It emphasizes great teaching, liberal arts orientation even in professional programs, and application-oriented research, distinguishing it from a university emphasizing theoretical research. Today it makes an ever-increasing contribution to the well-being of a metropolitan area of 2.75 million people. Its influence and service spread to all segments of the community and far beyond.

From 1966 to 1991 St. Thomas went through substantial growth and change. It grew from 2,167 to 10,500 students, from 1,900 to more than 5,000 undergraduate students. Enrollment in the graduate programs increased from 267 to more than 5,000.

The increase in physical facilities was also impressive. Where there had been one campus, there were now three. The value of the physical plant grew from $21 million to $170 million. Twenty-two buildings were constructed, acquired, or significantly added to during this period. An annual budget of $3.5 million was now well over $100 million. Endowment rose from $5.4 million to about $128 million.

There were many other areas of growth. With such an increase in student population, the number of employees went from 257 to 1,328, including from 136 faculty in 1966 to 578 in 1991. Salaries increased until they were truly competitive with outstanding institutions.

During this time the number of academic major fields available to undergraduate students on their home campus plus those available at the four neighboring colleges in the consortium known as the Associated Colleges of the Twin Cities (Macalester College, Hamline University, Augsburg College, and the College of St. Catherine) vastly increased. Two seminaries were added to prepare candidates for the priesthood. The college became coeducational. Thirteen major graduate programs and an evening college were created. A graduate school in business, with a master's in business administration as its centerpiece, was instituted and became the second largest such program in the United States. A master's degree in computer software and design enrolled five hundred students, probably the largest number of master's candidates in this discipline in the United States, perhaps in the world. The number of master-degree students in education reached fourteen hundred, likely the largest enrollment in such a program in the region. It has been estimated that ninety percent of the high schools in Minnesota had one or more faculty or staff members who had studied at the University of St. Thomas. Moreover, both undergraduate- and graduate-degree programs in social work were instituted.

Not just the broader community but also the church was served in new and important ways. Within the graduate school of education a program for independent schools prepared teachers and administrators for Catholic and other private schools. The school of divinity offered courses at the graduate level for the teachers and directors of parish religious education programs. One of the seminaries has college-level students. They take courses at the university but have a separate program of religious formation. The other has a four-year post-baccalaureate program in theology for ordination candidates.

Growth, whether in the number of students or buildings or programs or endowment, was not the objective. The goal was to bring the kind of religious, values-oriented education which St. Thomas provides to as many persons as possible and, in so doing, to enhance the lives of an ever increasing number of people. What brought about the development, what lay behind the numbers, was a very challenging mission and the commitment of the leadership to achieve the goals of the university. Mission, especially its religious dimension, and leadership were key factors.

The mission of St. Thomas includes a religious element as well as a liberal arts education and public service. All three reinforce one another and are closely related. The religious commitment is Catholic, yet similar in many ways to the religious commitment of many faiths. Its religious character is a dynamic element at the very core of the university, entering into the direction and energy of the institution. The mission was vitalized by a conviction that religion should play an influential role in the marketplace, in the total community.

For too long religion has been ignored and relegated solely to the private lives of people: their moral convictions were to be left at home and not influence their lives on the job, in community endeavors, or in their relationships with other people; merely "private feelings" should not be brought into classroom instruction. Such a philosophy impoverishes people's lives and undermines the health of society. For this reason, the conviction that religion should enter the marketplace and public forum became a guiding star that set the direction of the university.

The liberal arts—the second element in the mission statement—is a sort of ally of religious values. Their emphasis on the enduring values of civilized society are an important preparation for life. They give meaning to life and together with religion deal with the perennial problems of human existence. They are also an excellent preparation for careers in most fields, including education in the professions leading to the service of others.

Community service is a third priority in the mission of St. Thomas. It clearly relates to the liberal arts, and especially to religion, both in motivation and in service. St. Thomas increasingly emphasized service to the church and community by identifying needs and providing academic programs that met them. For example, there was one MBA (master of business administration) program in the metropolitan area; it had an enrollment of only two to three hundred students and was virtually limited to full-time day students. People with jobs had no opportunity to gain an advanced degree. St. Thomas designed an MBA program that was especially suited for them. It also identified other areas where needs existed and created programs to fill them, for example, in teacher education, social work, engineering, and computer software. Thus, it provided large numbers of people opportunities to further their education and to do so in a faith-oriented curriculum. In doing this, it grew from a college to a university and acquired a new and important role in the community.

A new kind of leadership emerged—entrepreneurial leadership. Leadership in educational institutions has traditionally been conservative, cautious, and willing to take but few risks. There are many reasons for this, including the personality profile of persons attracted to academic life. They place a high premium on security and predictability. Entrepreneurial leadership involves prudent risk-taking and a willingness and capability to grasp opportunities when they arise. An evolving mission and a new kind of leadership gave a dynamic quality to St. Thomas. It grew in size and spread its influence into new areas.

This book will look carefully at entrepreneurial leadership as an agent of change. The establishment of a new campus by a private university in the very center of a major city is an accomplishment deserving careful attention. It was perhaps the only new campus created by a private university in the heart of a large metropolitan area in twenty-five years. There is a considerable difference between maintaining or managing an existing university and creating a new university or new life for an existing institution. Both require excellent management and the handling of problems. New institutions, however, call for creativity, entrepreneurship, and risk-taking. These qualities are quite different from those needed to manage an ongoing institution.

In the process of looking at development in community involvement, it will be possible to gain a better understanding of the role religion can play in the life of a university and community. Since the religious character is seldom looked at as an active, dynamic element at the core of a university, entering into the direction and energy of the institution, it will be helpful to look at the role it has played at one institution as it grew rapidly and extended its service and influence. This study of the religious mission of a university will show how, under entrepreneurial leadership, religious values and commitment to the community played out in specific academic programs. These have a significant dimension not always found in similar programs, especially those in state universities, namely, a moral component and a vision of what constitutes a just and peaceful society.

Religion relates to all phases of one's life; hence, wherever possible, it should be integrated into the various subjects that are important to one's life and to society, into subjects that are frequently regarded as purely secular but which have a moral dimension that is often excluded. A university under Catholic auspices does not provide a Catholic education if it follows the secular pattern, even if it also sponsors extracurricular programs that help the needy and the unfortunate, important as such programs are. A Catholic university's curriculum should lead to an intellectual conviction of the moral values that are relevant to one's daily work, to responsible citizenship, and to the support of human dignity.

What Is Catholic about a Catholic University?

To understand religious convictions as part of the mission of a Catholic university, it is necessary to know how such an institution defines itself.[1] What are its mission and goals? Generally, church-related universities in America are based on Judeo-Christian traditions, and their values reflect these theological and philosophical positions. There are many degrees of commitment to these values. Catholic institutions usually go beyond the espousal of values and embrace a whole range of Christian teachings and practice. What then is a Catholic college or university? A Vatican document entitled *Ex Corde Ecclesiae* has spelled out the criteria to which a Catholic institution, if it wishes to be called Catholic, should conform.[2]

This document was the product of many conferences and of discussions among Catholic institutions and sometimes with church officials. The Second Vatican Council recognized that its "Declaration on Christian Education" did not speak to higher education.[3] Consequently, it

---

[1] In this book the word "university" generally includes undergraduate colleges as well as postbaccalaureate schools.

[2] John Paul II, Pope, *Apostolic Constitution* Ex Corde Ecclesiae *of the Supreme Pontiff John Paul II on Catholic Universities*, Origins 20 (4 October 1990).

[3] Vatican Council II, *Gravissimum Educationis*, Acta Apostolicae Sedis 58 (28 October 1965) 728; [Gravissimum Educationis: *Declaration on Christian Education*, in *The Basic Sixteen Documents: Constitutions, Decrees, Declarations*, ed. Austin Flannery (Northport, N.Y.: Costello, 1996)].

decided that the subject of Catholic higher education should be taken up later.

A word of explanation concerning the Second Vatican Council seems in order here. Pope John XXIII convened it and all the Catholic bishops of the world were expected to attend. The purpose of the council, which lasted from 1962 to 1965, was to "update" the church. Not since the Council of Trent in the sixteenth century has any event so profoundly changed the Catholic Church. It called for a new openness to the modern world; it challenged the church to be more fully engaged in all aspects of life and society; it also called for greater participation by lay people in the life of the church.

The invitation to Catholic higher education to write its own charter for Vatican approval ushered in a challenging and difficult process. At issue was the nature of a Catholic university and its relationship to the church. In the United States discussion took place within the context of the American juridical separation of church and state. Church-related institutions and their students needed and deserved the same kind of government financial assistance secular universities received. The line of separation between church and state could not be crossed. Yet where the line was could not always be easily determined. There were overzealous "defenders of the faith"—both faiths—religious faith and the secular faith of an absolute separation of church and state.

There was also the fact that American Catholic education wanted to be in the mainstream of higher education. Vatican II, with its characteristic openness, reinforced its position that Catholic colleges and universities should not be in a Catholic ghetto; they should welcome students and faculty from all persuasions. (A senior faculty member—a staunch defender of Catholic principles—remarked to this author that he found the presence of an agnostic colleague to be challenging, stimulating, and exciting.) Moreover, the universities need a broader base of financial support. Dioceses and religious orders cannot give sufficient help. As the number of religious declines, and therefore their contributed services also decline, and enrollments grow, additional outside financial assistance becomes ever more needed.

A dimension of the controversy is the Vatican's view that a Catholic university should be juridically related to the church. Its experience over the centuries when many European Catholic universities became secularized made it apprehensive lest the same fate befall the American universities. At the same time, many American educators thought the Vatican proposals did not reflect the American experience. The American tradition, and one insisted upon by accrediting associations, called for a high degree of autonomy and self-governance. Educators from countries with oppressive governments, such as Poland, welcomed a juridical bond to the church as a way of keeping the government at arm's length. But the European experience was not the same as the American experience.

Twenty-five years after the council, after much labor and controversy, the Holy See issued the Apostolic Constitution *Ex Corde Ecclesiae*. Because Catholic universities vary so widely, the criteria set forth as standards for Catholic colleges and universities are necessarily very general. The great national university of Louvain in Belgium differs greatly from Sophia University in Tokyo where perhaps only two or three percent of the faculty and staff is Catholic. Lublin University, in Poland and under Communist rule, differed considerably from a college for women in the United States. Broad sweeping criteria that cover such diverse situations tell little about the distinctive character of any university. Catholic universities vary greatly. Their basic characteristics as defined by *Ex Corde Ecclesiae* are:

1. A Christian inspiration not only of individuals, but also of the university community as such.

2. A continuing reflection in the light of the Catholic faith upon the growing treasury of human knowledge, to which it seeks to contribute by its own research.

3. Fidelity to the Christian message as it comes to us through the Church.

4. An institutional commitment to the service of the people of God and of the human family in their pilgrimage to the transcendent goal which gives meaning to life.[4]

Within this broad framework each institution develops in distinctive ways, depending on its sponsoring religious group, leadership, geo-

---

[4] *Ex Corde Ecclesiae,* par. 13. As broad as these criteria are, they may still present problems for some universities. In 1972, at the conclusion of a conference at the Vatican at which these criteria were originally presented, this author asked a representative from an Asian country what was his opinion of the criteria and the document that contained them. He replied that they might be all right on the president's desk, but not beyond that. In his institution the faculty and student body were almost entirely non-Christian.

graphical and demographic situation, cultural environment, institutional history, faculty and student body.

In a Catholic institution theology should hold an important place in the curriculum. To be truly Catholic, it is not enough for a university to provide a religious environment and worship opportunities. A Catholic university should provide courses in theology that are theologically sound, well-taught, and conform to rigorous academic standards. The theology faculty should have training and degrees at least equal to those of other faculties in the university. Students today come to college with little or no theological education; so even at the college level there is need for introductory courses. After students have acquired a basic knowledge of theology, they may go on to examine various theological systems, but it is unproductive to attempt such an examination before the students have at least a rudimentary knowledge of theology.

If one shifts the question from "What is a Catholic university?" to "What is a Catholic education?" it is clear that instruction in the Catholic faith is essential. Education is essentially an intellectual exercise and the Catholic dimension of it must also have an intellectual activity. Worship and religious devotions are certainly important in Catholic life, but they alone, even when conducted on a Catholic campus, are not sufficient to provide a Catholic education. The same is also true, perhaps even more so, in regard to many social-action programs: these raise consciousness regarding the needs of society and educate the conscience; they can provide contact with social issues and with marginalized people which students will remember for a lifetime. It can be argued that such studies and activities give specificity to the humanities and theology.

However, as valuable as all these are, they do not, of themselves, constitute a Catholic education. For that, intellectual understanding of core Catholic beliefs is necessary. Hence, courses in theology are essential elements in Catholic education. Other things, such as worship and social action, are complementary to education in the Catholic intellectual tradition.

Ex Corde Ecclesiae often speaks of Catholic education enhancing "human dignity" through the advancement of "cultural progress," the promotion of justice, peace, political order, and economic opportunities and development. The more one becomes capable of using one's God-given intelligence, the more evident the divine stamp of the Creator becomes. One very essential contribution to "human dignity" is educating people to think critically and constructively. The development of the mind, of the ability to think, to grasp principles, to analyze, to think creatively, to know how to proceed in mastering a subject, is a basic aim of liberal arts education. It is also one of the greatest things that can be done to enhance human dignity. This kind of intellectual development is also a great aid in the study of theology. It enables a person to deal with the changing currents in theology and to confront the ever new developments in society from a theological perspective.

Catholic colleges have long stressed the liberal arts, which constitute a matrix for answers to the perennial questions of human existence. The study of the whole human enterprise, with its struggle to accentuate all that is truly human and elevating and meaningful, gives a better understanding of humanity fallen and yet redeemed. It liberates and opens the mind to growth and the understanding of one's condition and that of one's fellow human beings and in the process to the laying hold of the values that are truly worthwhile and enduring. The breadth of a liberal arts education is a wonderful preparation for living a meaningful life.

This cultivation of human intelligence and the enhancement of human dignity are invaluable contributions that a Catholic university makes. The theological dimension of a Catholic education gives a broader perspective and therefore contributes to the development of the person. It is a basic contribution a Catholic liberal arts education makes to its students. One can easily overlook the significance of this contribution when one is looking at other studies that may be more glamorous and eye-catching at the moment. However, this contribution is a distinctive feature of Catholic colleges and universities in the United States because the foundation of it is done in the first two years, especially in the core curriculum. Often European universities begin with the more specialized studies that American colleges take up in the last two years of study.

For a religious university, service to the community is a response to the scriptural mandate to love one's neighbor. The companion commandment is to love God. These are the basis of service to others. There are many aspects or ways that a university can serve and give glory to God.

At the core of the Christian Catholic faith is the belief that the human person was created in the image of God. God became incarnate in the person of Jesus Christ. In so doing, the incarnation gave an added dimension to human dignity: the human person would never be the same. A new challenge had been given, namely, to create a society worthy of redeemed men and women, one in which the human potential could be fully realized. To the extent that a university enables people to become fully alive, to activate all their potential, to develop all their God-given talents, to that extent it furthers the purpose for which God created the world and became incarnate. In the words of St. Irenaeus, the human person fully alive is the glory of God. The Christian mysteries of birth (Christmas) and resurrection (Easter) have special meaning for Christian colleges and universities, for they give added meaning to the purpose for which these schools exist. They are the basis for incarnational studies.

When God became incarnate, a whole new level of human dignity became possible. The work of the Catholic university is to enhance human dignity and therefore to carry out the enhancement begun at Bethlehem. Amid all the failures and discouragements of individuals and societies, hope that ultimately goodness and truth will prevail is an important virtue. The resurrection of Jesus is the basis for the Christian virtue of hope and confidence. It gives confidence that the intellectual enterprise is worthwhile, worth all the effort and sacrifice because it will endure and benefit the human race. Ultimately rationality and goodness will prevail. The enhancement of human dignity is a fundamental contribution a Catholic university can make to the community.

Cardinal Newman, in a famous sermon, spoke of intellectual excellence and moral (will) excellence as united before the Fall, described in Genesis. After the Fall they tend to separate: "The grace is gone; the soul cannot hold together; it falls to pieces; its elements strive with each other. . . ."[5] Later on in the same sermon he stated the purpose of a Catholic university: "Here, then, I conceive, is the object of the . . . Catholic Church in setting up Universities; it is to reunite things which were in the beginning joined together by God, and not put asunder by man. . . . I wish the same spots and the same individuals to be at once oracles of philosophy and shrines of devotion. . . . I want the intellectual layman to be religious, and the devout ecclesiastic to be intellectual."[6] The pursuit of knowledge and moral excellence, with God's grace, can give a wholeness to a person and etch more clearly the image of God which includes the whole person, body as well as soul.

This view is clearly expressed in the American bishops' pastoral letter entitled "Catholic Higher Education and the Pastoral Mission of the Church": "Human culture is good to the extent that it reflects the plan

---

[5] John Henry Newman, *Sermons Preached on Various Occasions* (London: Longmans, Green, 1894) 6.

[6] Ibid., 13.

and purpose of the Creator, but it bears the wounds of sin. The Church wishes to make the Gospel of Jesus Christ present to the world and to every sector of humanity at every stage of history. The Catholic college or university seeks to do this by educating men and women to play responsible roles in the contemporary world in the framework of that most important historical fact: the sending of the Son by the Father to reconcile, to vivify, to spread the Good News, to call all the world to a restoration in Christ Jesus."[7] This is very close to Pope John Paul II's statement: "All the basic academic activities of a Catholic university are connected with and in harmony with the evangelizing mission of the Church. . . ."[8]

Catholicism is concerned with the ultimate questions of human existence, such questions as the meaning of human life; the what, where, why, and how of our existence; good and evil; the meaning, significance, and source of the whole human enterprise, and the source of life and all things. These questions occur to reflective people. Catholic education should help students to address them and—in some measure—find answers to them. Such questions arise in many disciplines, but the answers are often to be sought outside the confines of a narrow academic discipline. Philosophy and theology deal with some of these questions, but other disciplines, such as history and literature, have something to say about them as well. This is not to suggest that academic disciplines which fail to address such questions are inferior to theology in a curriculum. Rather, it may mean that, because the methodology used is different from theology's, the result is different or, perhaps, that there are restraints, external to the discipline, imposed by society. In a religiously oriented university it is easier to identify and deal with such questions because they have an essential religious dimension. In a university which is avowedly secular, it is more difficult to confront them openly.

One might argue that philosophy, which is based on reason, rather than theology, which is based on divine revelation, is more naturally related to the other academic disciplines. However, Christian philosophy and theology are related, although distinct, subjects. Both point to the underlying theories and principles of every area of study. They appertain to the ultimate significance of each discipline in itself and in relation to other fields. Historically, Christian philosophy and theology

[7] "Catholic Higher Education and the Pastoral Mission of the Church," *Origins* 10 (13 November 1980) 378–79.

[8] *Ex Corde Ecclesiae*, par. 49.

have developed in relation to each other, and together they are essential to Christian wisdom. Ideally, the Christian university enables students to glimpse wisdom and strive to attain it; such wisdom is attainable when philosophy and theology play their rightful roles. And wisdom ultimately leads to the Risen Christ and his plan for humankind.

4

Catholic Studies in Relation to Other Studies

Theology must be in a dynamic relationship with other disciplines in a university. Catholic theology embraces a worldview. It has a particular way of looking at reality, at human existence, at its significance and meaning. All aspects of reality should be seen in their totality and this includes the religious dimension. Each discipline taught in a university pertains to a slice of reality and very frequently that piece has a relationship to theology. It is therefore better understood, more completely grasped, if its religious dimension is included. This is especially true in the social sciences and the humanities where knowledge of human nature is essential for understanding the subject. Social behavior, literature, economic decisions, political actions are but a few of the areas of study where human nature is at the very center. One's view of human nature, whether Christian, materialistic, positivistic, humanistic, Marxist, or mechanistic, conditions one's study and one's conclusions. The theological and philosophical dimensions can be dismissed only at the price of diminishing understanding.

John Henry Newman, the great proponent of liberal education, never spoke of theology as the capstone in a hierarchy of knowledge. Unlike medievalists who saw theology as the "queen of the sciences" and at the top of a pyramid of knowledge, ruling other disciplines, Newman always used the image of a circle made up of a variety of subjects, including theology, which are interdependent. He spoke of each study's having its proper place in the universe of knowledge.[1]

A Catholic university has the advantage of being able to espouse a religious or philosophical position while also examining carefully other views and stating their positions clearly. As long as it openly avows its position, is willing to have it scrutinized by any and all, and is tolerant of views held by others, it can provide a distinctive kind of education.

Through specialization modern scholarship has made tremendous advances in knowledge. More and more areas of study are dividing into sub-specialties. The various fields claim autonomy; they stand alone enjoying almost complete independence. There is considerable merit in such specialization. It brings about more specific and detailed knowledge. There are also some dangers, such as an intellectual narrowness. This can be a problem, especially in religious liberal arts universities where intellectual breadth is important. The relationship of a discipline to cognate areas, including religious and moral values, is an integral element of education. Extreme specialization may squeeze out such considerations.

In addition to problems resulting from specialization, there is the added problem that much graduate education professedly omits any consideration of a theological nature. Many graduates of such education do not see any relevance of theology or ethics to their field. This is often not a question of hostility to religion but rather a lack of knowledge. Sometimes there is a concern that integrating philosophical or theological considerations with another discipline may scare off some persons.

Certainly religion should not be introduced where it is not relevant. Such action would undermine both subjects. The first requirement is good education. The integrity and validity of each academic discipline must be respected. A university must be an excellent academic institution before it is an excellent Catholic school. If it fails to provide a superior education, it fails to be a good Catholic university. The presence of a Catholic commitment can never substitute for academic excellence. Conversely, the exclusion of relevant religious considerations diminishes academic quality.

[1] Ian Ker, noted Newman scholar, has written, "It should, however, be noted that far from ever speaking of a 'hierarchy' of branches of knowledge, Newman's favoured image is the circle which is intended to imply interdependence not equality, since certain key branches of knowledge like ethics and theology . . . impinge upon (not rule over) a number of other branches of knowledge." Ian Ker, *John Henry Newman* (New York: Oxford University Press, 1990) 392.

The inner logic, the prevailing norms of a discipline, its way of proceeding, its methods and findings must all be respected. Other disciplines should be heard only when they are relevant and enriching. This implies that there be no a priori exclusion of considerations from another field of study, but rather an openness to all fields that can be helpful. At the same time, Catholic theology and philosophy must be careful not to encroach upon other subjects. They need to "get inside" a related field in order to understand it before bringing forth proposals.

This touches upon a central problem of Catholic higher education: how to relate Catholic theology to other disciplines, given the departmentalization that has become a standard in higher education and given the secularization of many graduate schools. The ideal solution would be to hire faculty proficient in their fields and knowledgeable in philosophy and theology. The experience of the University of St. Thomas is instructive. Despite constant effort over many years, relatively few such persons were available. To hire at least one person in each department who is knowledgeable in the Catholic intellectual tradition as well as in his/her academic discipline and who can help colleagues to understand that tradition, is a worthy and perhaps attainable goal. In addition to trying to hire knowledgeable people, St. Thomas developed programs to assist faculty who wish to learn more about religion and in relation to their field of study. Summer workshops have been very helpful and sabbaticals for research in the religious and value dimension of a discipline are also advantageous. However, financial assistance is vital in this area of faculty development.

George Marsden lists a number of recognized scholars whose writings have "substantial Christian perspectives." He then goes on to cite various organizations and societies that encourage scholarly work with a religious dimension. In order to be as specific as possible, he cites ongoing work in several fields. All of this is evidence of the possibility and advantage of Christian research and publishing.[2] However, one of the difficulties scholars, especially young scholars, face when they want to do research and write in a religious vein is the lack of financial support. That may be changing as foundations such as the Lilly and Pew foundations support some religious endeavors in the field of education. Beyond the financial obstacles, there lurks the reception such work might

---

[2] See George M. Marsden, *The Outrageous Idea of Christian Scholarship* (New York: Oxford University Press, 1997) 113–19.

receive in promotion and tenure committees, even the reaction doctoral candidates might encounter if they propose a thesis subject having a religious dimension.

A fundamental question is whether a distinctively Catholic education is possible today: Is it really possible to achieve the religious goals of a university in a pluralistic society which demands that hiring practices reflect the various groups or elements in that society? Within search committees, advocates of certain causes can be so vociferous that they drown out any consideration of the mission of a university. The weight of government programs and laws runs against considering religion in hiring practices except perhaps in hiring faculty for a theology department and a few key administrative positions.

A Catholic university should welcome the presence of persons of persuasions different from its formal commitment as long as it is not hindered in hiring at least enough people who understand and can communicate its positions in those areas where the gospel is relevant. The important thing is that Catholic values and principles be adequately presented wherever they are relevant.

The question may be asked: Whose theology? Differences in theological matters within the church are sometimes cited as obstacles to integrating theology with other disciplines. Yet there have always been differences within a basic unity. One need only recall those between St. Peter and St. Paul in regard to the observance of Jewish laws and customs on the part of Gentile converts. Down through the ages the great religious communities such as Dominicans, Franciscans, Jesuits, and Benedictines have held differing theological positions. So it is to be expected that today, following Vatican II, there are different views on church matters. It can be a sign of health. Unhappily it is sometimes used as an excuse for not confronting forthrightly the relation between theology and another discipline.

The chief providers of a Catholic education are the faculty. No amount of rhetoric from the president's office, or statements of mission, or religious symbols, helpful as these may be, constitute a Catholic university or a Catholic education. What goes on in the classroom day after day determines whether or not the educational experience has a religious or value dimension. The faculty is the key. They must understand the religious element of the mission of the university.

Ex Corde Ecclesiae recommends that at least a majority of the faculty be Catholic. However, a formal profession of faith on the part of Catholic faculty members does not insure that they understand the Catholic intellectual tradition and values pertinent to their academic discipline. Even graduate education at a Catholic university gives no assurance that the faculty member knows the Catholic tradition or how a particular area of study relates to that tradition. For example, in many Catholic universities, business, management, and economics attract a large number of students. In fact, business and management may well be the largest departments. Yet many faculty members are not prepared to teach business ethics or Catholic social doctrine.

The Catholic tradition in business matters really goes back to the Book of Genesis, as Pope John Paul II has stated. In the early church and in the Middle Ages, theologians and preachers wrote and spoke on such matters as fair wages and just prices. Certainly Thomas Aquinas wrote on such matters. In modern times, at least for the last one hundred years, there has been a stream of papal announcements on socio-economic matters, and these have been followed by scholarly commentaries as well as local and regional episcopal statements. This tradition is cited as a body of teaching pertinent to a major and popular academic discipline, one that pertains to the livelihood of many students, sometimes the majority.

What can be done to insure that students are made acquainted with this tradition? At St. Thomas there is an ongoing program of teaching business ethics to faculty and enabling them to include ethics in their business classes wherever it is relevant. In addition, administrative leadership must endeavor to hire a sufficient number of people who are conversant in the Catholic intellectual tradition. It is too much to expect today that every faculty member of a university will become well-versed in such matters, but it is not too much to expect all faculty members to respect the tradition. It is not too much to expect a university to have a solid core of faculty well-trained in Catholic thought. These can have enormous impact on the student body and make the religious dimension of a university a living reality.

In 1994, St. Thomas instituted the Center for Catholic Studies to relate theology and a number of other academic areas in a more formal way. It brings together faculty members from various fields who are prepared to teach courses that relate their discipline to theology. For example, a professor in the English department might teach a course on the Catholic novel in which he/she would analyze religious themes which play an important part in a story. The religious element might not be explicit but is nonetheless present and meaningful. Other fields of study present similar opportunities for a deeper and more thorough understanding when their theological-philosophical dimensions are made more explicit, in psychology, sociology, and biology for instance.

The Center for Catholic Studies, as distinct from the Catholic theology department, offers an academic major which consists of several courses in theology (in addition to those required of all students) and other courses that explore the relationship between theology and other academic fields. Some examples are Science and Christian Theology, Christian Faith and the Management Profession, Psychology and the Moral Life, Wholeness and Holiness. This program is very popular with students, as can be seen from its rapid growth in enrollment. There is also an indirect, but very important, effect of this program. Faculty who teach in it, who spend their time studying the religious connections of their discipline, undoubtedly influence others in their field to look at the religious dimensions of the subject matter, something that was neglected in their graduate studies.

The center is cited as an example of the beneficial results from the long-running dialogue between church officials and educators. That dialogue was a learning experience for both sides, and it challenged universities to find ways to live out their Catholic commitments. A number of universities have inaugurated new programs to emphasize their Catholic identity, which became a topic of considerable discussion, especially under the leadership of the Association of Catholic Colleges and Universities. A few years ago fifty-seven persons representing thirty leading institutions met at the Gainey Conference Center of the University of St. Thomas to share with one another their programs designed to integrate Catholic culture and theology with the rest of their curricula.

While *Ex Corde Ecclesiae* did not lay to rest all the concerns of educators, it was widely heralded as an inspiring and encouraging document. Furthermore, it gave a sense of direction and guidance. Clearly, progress had been made toward the goal of the church's understanding of its colleges and universities, a goal envisaged by the Second Vatican Council when it set aside its efforts to write a document on higher education and encouraged Catholic educators to study the matter further. This unfinished business of Vatican II was both an opportunity and a challenge which the Catholic universities responded to faithfully and creatively.

The challenges and opportunities in society and in the church in the last half of the twentieth century revealed the fundamental importance of religion as a dimension of higher education. Their Catholicism is a great asset of Catholic universities, and rather than downplay it under the influence of the secular culture, they should see it as a great and distinctive strength. What is required is a recognition of the values of Catholicism in education and a sustained effort to integrate them into the curriculum and other phases of university life. Catholicism is not an appendix, not just an ally, but a constitutive element of Catholic higher education. Catholic universities should be very clear in setting it forth as a strength.

Some years ago, when this author talked about teaching business ethics, some faculty members worried that businesses would not be interested in it and dismiss it as "a Catholic concern." The opposite occurred: business leaders of all religious persuasions responded very favorably. They welcomed it and welcomed employees whose education included a concern for ethics. What was thought to be something negative was shown to be a great asset.

St. Thomas must deal with certain contentions raised from time to time. One such contention pertains to academic freedom, the foundation stone of modern intellectual academic life: Is academic freedom compatible with the claims of Catholicism? Can St. Thomas adhere to Catholic teachings as its mission statement asserts and yet be committed to academic freedom?

Cases such as that of Charles Curran give rise to concern about whether any Catholic university truly believes in, or has the liberty to uphold, academic freedom.[3] In addition, the history of the Inquisition raises fears about freedom in Catholic institutions. At St. Thomas, there has never been a denial of academic freedom. Yet one should not dismiss this concern out of hand. It can trouble people outside the university. On at least two occasions the fear that academic freedom might not be observed was an important factor in the breakdown of discussions on mergers between the University of St. Thomas and a complementary institution. Despite repeated assurances that academic freedom would be respected and despite the fact that in its more than one hundred years of existence St. Thomas has never had a case of the denial of aca-

---

[3] Father Charles Curran was a tenured member of the theology faculty of the Catholic University of America in Washington, D.C. In 1986 the Vatican Congregation for the Doctrine of the Faith said he was no longer "suitable nor eligible to teach Catholic theology." On April 12, 1988, the board of trustees of Catholic University withdrew his church license to teach theology but said he retained his tenure outside the university's theology school, which was accredited by the Vatican. He was judged unfit to teach theology "because of his dissent from Church teachings on certain moral issues." *Origins* 17 (21 April 1988) 758.

demic freedom, this objection rose so often that even some fellow members on the same side as the objectors were embarrassed. No amount of assurance could persuade the latter.

John Milton is often cited on intellectual freedom. Milton thought that if every idea could be freely expressed, no matter how outrageous, the truest views would prevail. Rational people would weigh them all and the most valid and reasonable ideas would prevail. It is a sort of Darwinian concept, that is, the strongest and fittest would survive. Competition among intellectual positions assure, so it is argued, that the reasonable positions survive while the unreasonable do not. Milton's idea of a free marketplace of competitive ideas is still valid. However, in a world of mass communication the outcome often depends on who the proponents of various positions are, how capable they are, what means of communication are at their disposal. Analogously, the ideas which prevail in academia may depend on who supports them and what their resources are.

In a Catholic university any position that is intellectually valid should be allowed. Discussion of what can or cannot be taught is irrelevant, and there should be no question about academic freedom.[4] But a Catholic university should claim that the Catholic position be given a fair hearing. The burden of having people capable of articulating this tradition falls on the faculty and administration of the university itself. So the appropriate question is not about academic freedom; the appropriate question is about whether the Catholic view is competently, fairly, and articulately presented. If it is, then Catholic thought can expect to have a respectful hearing in the marketplace of ideas both within and without academia.

---

[4] A more thorough treatment of academic freedom is beyond the scope of this presentation. There is, for example, a distinction to be made between the academic presentation of a position in all its intellectual strength and the advocacy of a position. The latter moves beyond the realms of ideas and into the field of action and therefore beyond the guidelines of good teaching. This distinction may, at times, be difficult to apply in practice. Some positions that are clearly immoral, such as hatred and racism, are not entitled to academic protection. Likewise, good teaching requires, among other things, that consideration be given to the intellectual level of the student and the relevancy of the topic to the discipline being taught. And some might argue that in a Catholic university Catholic teaching should have a special status, a sort of position of honor. For an informative treatment of academic freedom in a Catholic university, see William J. Byron, S.J., *Quadrangle Considerations* (Chicago: Loyola University Press, 1989) 29–51.

An example of a failure to deal adequately with a Catholic position occurred when the bishops of the United States published a draft of their pastoral letter on the American economy, *Economic Justice For All.*[5] A public forum was held on the St. Thomas campus. Representative faculty from the social sciences made up a panel to discuss it. The panelists looked at the document from the viewpoint of their own specialty, whereas the document was interdisciplinary and concerned with policy questions which transcend a single academic discipline. It also had a substantial moral content. No one came forward to discuss the document on its own terms, that is, within the tradition out of which this document on the economy and public policy was written. In this case, the faculty of a Catholic institution did not present a Catholic position on a very important subject—the country's economy. The fault was the university's, both faculty and administrators, for it failed to engage at least some people who were knowledgeable in Catholic social thought. Since then there has been renewed emphasis on Catholic social teaching. A chair in business ethics has been established as well as a program to bring ethics into all phases of business education. Catholic social principles are now taught across the curriculum.

From the point of view of the total development of the student, the correlation between the study of the field in which they are likely to earn a living and their theological-philosophical tradition gives a sense of personal integrity, of wholeness. There should be no artificial separation between one's job and the rest of one's life. This unity can come about if religious and ethical values are seen as relevant to the marketplace and to the totality of life and if the education provided links values and work.

In a modern Catholic university there will be people of various religious persuasions and of no persuasion. The convictions of all must be respected, and they should expect the Catholic intellectual tradition to be respected and presented as well. Students and faculty may or may not be persuaded by Catholic values and principles. Their acceptance or rejection is a matter of their intellect and conscience. They must be free to assent to or to ignore. So also the Catholic university must be free to teach its intellectual tradition.

---

[5] National Council of Catholic Bishops, *Economic Justice for All: Catholic Social Teaching and the U.S. Economy, Origins* 16 (27 November 1986) 1ff.

5

A Catholic University Reaches Out

There are many ways in which a church-related university can help its students relate their lives to their religious and moral convictions and to the service of the community. Concern for the environment is one example, for there is a profound religious base for the careful stewardship of our world.

A Christian university has an excellent opportunity to contribute to the wise use of the earth. It trains people in a whole range of natural and social sciences that bear upon economic and cultural development. Biology, chemistry, and geology have much to contribute to the proper use of the earth's resources. Economics, political science, and ethics are keys to the conditions that enable free and creative people to multiply the goods of the earth so as to sustain a high level of well-being and culture and yet not deplete our natural resources. Religion should enhance the motivation to preserve the earth.

Today, many people are concerned about the environment. Waste, the thinning of the ozone layer, landfill limits, extinction of species, environmental pollution, depletion of natural resources, especially of energy, are very much on the minds of young people. So it is not surprising that there should have been a strong interest in the environment among St. Thomas students as well as faculty. The establishment of an academic major in environmental studies flowed naturally and easily out of efforts on the part of faculty in departments which have a relationship to the environment. The full faculty readily approved an interdisciplinary program in environmental studies which integrated the natural and social sciences. Student enrollment was immediately strong, and the first group of majors graduated in the spring of 1994.

The environmental program had a natural relation to another St. Thomas program which involved students from kindergarten through high school: the World School for Adventure Learning related youths' interest in adventure to concern for the environment. It followed the trail of Will Steger, renowned Arctic and Antarctic explorer and author, during his trip to the North Pole. He reported daily to the World School on the St. Thomas campus which, in turn, disseminated the information to more than three hundred schools and school systems. The number of students reached worldwide was estimated at over one million. Teachers in the schools were able to contact the World School with questions, and both St. Thomas faculty and students majoring in environmental studies supplied the answers. In addition, grade and high schools organized environmental activities in their own areas, such as studying lakes and streams, the runoff of chemicals from lawns, the protection of wetlands, so that youngsters would relate study and action. The motto of the program was that of the environmental movement: "Think globally, act locally."

Religious motivation can be a powerful incentive for good stewarding of the earth's resources. The Book of Genesis relates that the Creator gave men and women the charge to act responsibly with the goods of the earth as God's partners in continuing creation. If they do so intelligently and responsibly, the earth can support the human race from generation to generation. Clearly, there are starving people on this earth. The answer to the problem of hunger lies in the creative and entrepreneurial spirit of men and women. Human resources and natural resources need to be employed in ways that maximize both; the right political and economic systems need to be in place in order for the earth to be sufficiently bountiful not only to feed the world's population but also to enable it to enjoy a reasonable level of culture.

Human beings are unquestionably the most important ingredient in raising the standard of living. Holland and Belgium are good examples of countries with limited natural resources, but the right human resources as well as free political and economic systems make it possible for them to support a high standard of living for relatively large populations. On the opposite side, Brazil and Argentina have great natural resources but dismal records after World War II in using their God-given resources. Their populations, many of whom are drawn from the industrial nations of Europe, would seemingly have the ability to develop their countries; however, for a long time they lacked democratic political systems and free economies—both essential elements for development.

In all of this, people working hand-in-hand with the Creator become co-creators: God's plan for the earth and its people is furthered. Universities which succeed in giving their students a sense of responsibility for the preservation and development of the earth in the service of humankind confer an inestimable benefit on their students and on the human family. In so doing, they raise the level of idealism and the satisfaction that comes from a significant accomplishment in the service of a noble endeavor. For what could give greater satisfaction than the awareness that one's daily task in earning a living contributes to the glory of God and the betterment of one's neighbor?

Another program that excites young people as well as older people is peace and justice studies. Vatican II put great emphasis on peace and social justice, especially in the *Pastoral Constitution on the Church in the Modern World*.[1] Moreover, there has been a long tradition of Catholic social thought that, in its modern form, goes back at least one hundred years. Just before Vatican II, Pope John XXIII published his encyclical, entitled *Mater Et Magistra*, on social progress.[2] During the council he published another letter, *Pacem In Terris*.[3] Both won immediate acclaim. Their humanistic tone and broad social outreach found favor among people of all faiths. Following the council, the Vatican, in its efforts to implement the conciliar decrees, established within the Vatican the Office of Peace and Justice. More recently, Pope John Paul II's encyclical *Centesimus Annus*, with its balanced view of production and distribution, has become another foundational document for peace and justice efforts.[4]

At the University of St. Thomas an academic program on peace and justice was established in 1987. St. Thomas had a long and continuous history of concern for social justice. One of its early students was Monsignor John A. Ryan, who became the father of the social justice movement

[1] Vatican Council II, *Pastoral Constitution on the Church in the Modern World,* in *The Documents of Vatican II,* ed. Walter Abbott (New Century, 1966).

[2] John XXIII, Pope, *Mater et Magistra, Acta Apostolicae Sedis* 53 (1961); [*Mater et Magistra,* trans. William J. Gibbons (New York, Paulist Press, 1962)].

[3] John XXIII, Pope, *Pacem in Terris, Acta Apostolicae Sedis* 55 (1963); [*Pacem in Terris* (Washington, D.C.: National Catholic Welfare Conference, 1963)].

[4] John Paul II, Pope, *Centesimus Annus (On the Hundredth Anniversary of* Rerum Novarum*), Origins* 21 (16 May 1991) 1ff.

in the American Catholic Church, and down through the years St. Thomas had a long list of faculty who taught courses involving matters pertaining to justice and peace. The immediate occasion for establishing a new program was the pastoral letter of the American Catholic bishops entitled *The Challenge of Peace: God's Promise and Our Response,* published in 1986.[5]

The initiative came from the faculty. The president appointed a faculty-staff committee to study the feasibility of establishing a program and recommending its goals and curriculum. By 1987 the faculty had approved an academic field which grew into an academic major and became known as Justice and Peace Studies. Its goals are to prepare students to understand societies in order to improve them and to promote peace. The curriculum puts emphasis on nonviolence, on conflict resolution, on security and peace. Courses on the theologies of justice in society are required.

Throughout, and this is a distinguishing characteristic, emphasis is put on action. Firsthand experience of poverty and understanding its causes are intended to prepare students to become active workers for social improvement. Another important feature is its interfaith and interdisciplinary character designed to give an understanding of diverse cultures, philosophies, and worldviews.

The new program fits very naturally into the University of St. Thomas. Its religious and moral content, its concern for community, its pioneering programs for peace, its ecumenical efforts, all these recommended it to the entire faculty, which accepted it enthusiastically. It grew out of many interests of the faculty. It has enabled several disciplines such as biology, economics, environmental studies, geography, political science, and sociology to participate. All in all, the decision to establish it was an easy decision and a good example of collegial decision making.

Another dimension of the modern Church that finds a welcome home in a Catholic university and prepares young people for the kind of world in which they will live is ecumenism. Again, since Vatican II ecumenism has come of age. Now most dioceses have an office of ecumenism that promotes contacts, discussions, and prayer between churches. Catholic universities have a unique role to play in the effort to bring churches closer together. Historically, great theological issues have di-

---

[5] National Council of Catholic Bishops, *The Challenge of Peace: God's Promise and Our Response: A Pastoral Letter on War and Peace, Origins* 13 (19 May 1983) 1ff.

vided churches, but in recent years theologians have explored these issues to separate them from their historical setting, to find points of agreement, to clarify where there is real disagreement, and to continue study in an effort to come to some agreement. For the most part, Catholic theologians engaged in such endeavors are based in institutions of higher learning.

An important role for universities is to provide a place for church groups and others to come together for a variety of common purposes. People must work together to develop greater acceptance and friendship for one another. For a long time, Catholic universities have been members of many higher education organizations. In Minnesota the private church-related colleges banded together fifty years ago in the Minnesota Private College Council and Private College Fund. The council brings its collegiate members together on common concerns, especially those that relate to public policies and legislation. Together the presidents of the colleges began to call upon businesses to present the case for their institutions in seeking financial support. The president of a Catholic college, teamed up with his/her counterpart in a Protestant college, taught corporate donors lessons in religious cooperation. Such ventures also developed friendships between the presidents and this, in turn, brought closer collaboration among their faculties and administrators. Many common endeavors resulted. One very notable result of these is the consortium known as the Associated Colleges of the Twin Cities. Students may take courses on any of the five campuses. Another is the association of college libraries known as College Libraries in Consortium, which enables its nine participating institutions to share their library resources for the benefit of their faculties and students.

At the University of St. Thomas there has been a significant diversification of the faculty and student body. Historically, both were almost entirely Catholic. Now the number of Catholics in the undergraduate student body is about sixty percent. There are no satisfactory statistics on the religious preference of the faculty, but it is quite clear that the faculty is about evenly divided between non-Catholics and Catholics. While this has the advantage of giving students an experience which more nearly reflects the religious makeup of the environment in which they will earn a living, it leaves the university with the challenge to maintain its Catholic identity in a religiously diverse milieu. Yet this, too, is part of a pluralistic society.

A great contribution the church in America has made to the Universal Church is its example of living successfully and confidently in a religiously pluralistic society. The church survived and grew in a religiously hostile environment in early America. Now it is showing it can do well in a secular pluralistic society. What is needed now is a theology of the church in such a society. At Vatican II an American, John Courtney Murray, S.J., led the way in the work on the document on religious freedom, which represented a major shift in the position of the church from its historical preference for formal relations between church and state which included a preferential position for the Catholic Church, to one of equality for all churches, to a neutrality but not indifference on the part of the state to religion.

It seems clear that the twenty-first century will see a worldwide growth in the position which the Catholic Church in the United States has come to appreciate through experience. Catholic universities can lead the way, because of their experience and reflection, in this evolution, which found acceptance at Vatican II but still awaits a great deal of development, especially in the theology of religious pluralism.

This is a good example of a development in which experience precedes scholarship. It is theology from the bottom up. First, there is the lived experience of a free society and of the church within such a society; next there must follow a theological articulation of this experience. Only then will there be mutual benefit for the church and society: both will come to know themselves and each other better and be able to enrich one another. Pluralism and diversity are not the same, at least as diversity is sometimes presented, where diversity is taken to mean that any and every position can claim a legitimate and equal place in the curriculum. Such diversity can easily lead to a characterless smorgasbord presented as a curriculum. Pluralism, on the other hand, has room for differing views but maintains a central core of shared and tested convictions. Church-related universities must maintain their identity if they are not to become institutions of colorless secularism.

One of the very successful ventures in ecumenism at the University of St. Thomas is the Jay Phillips Center for Jewish-Christian Learning. It brings together Jewish and Christian scholars to discuss religious matters. The initiative for this program came from outside the university: two friends, one a Catholic member of the board of trustees, the other a recent president of the congregation of a synagogue, suggested to the president of the university that a Jewish-Christian dialogue be undertaken at St. Thomas. To develop understanding of the possibilities of such a program, a group was formed to visit Israel, concentrating on the places and activities that were especially meaningful for Jews; they also went to the Vatican and conferred with officials active in promoting Jewish-Catholic relations and met with Pope John Paul II.

St. Thomas was in a good position to undertake a program of Jewish-Christian studies. It had long had Jewish students, alumni, and faculty —although there never were many at any one time—and the attitude was always cordial. Also, some members of the theological faculty had done extensive Jewish studies. Supporting all this was the papal document, *Nostra Aetate,* which encouraged Jewish-Catholic initiatives.[6] In addition, St. John's University in Collegeville, Minnesota, had inaugurated the Jay Phillips Chair in Jewish Studies in 1969, the first such chair in the United States, and in July 1996 the two universities combined their programs and the holder of the chair, Rabbi Barry Cytron, was appointed full-time director.

The center's phenomenal success, judged by attendance at its lectures and discussions, is based in great part on the fact that it concentrates on religious matters, not in any polemical way, but rather in a neighborly way of explaining one's self and one's convictions to another, nor does it dwell on political or social issues. However, before these last can be addressed in a productive way, there must be an understanding of their relation to Judaism and Christianity. And there is indeed a deep desire on the part of Jews and Christians to understand and to share the religious teachings of each other. Topics such as prayer, the meaning of covenant, the life and meaning of Jesus, have attracted great attention. The publication of the papers presented at these forums has received attention around the world. Moreover, an outgrowth of the center's work is the offering of undergraduate courses on Judaism, which are very well attended, as well as the establishment of an interfaith library within the university's library system. Another valuable development is a program with the university's theologate which enables Catholic seminarians to study in Israel and meet Israeli families.

In a modern society, a pluralistic one, a Catholic university should be a place where the church and culture meet. It should provide a place where the church can reflect on the various aspects of the culture in which it finds itself, the better to adopt the culture's good points and to share its own values, principles, and worldview with it. In this way a Catholic university can greatly enhance the inculturation of the church,

---

[6] Paul VI, Pope, Nostra Aetate: *Declaration on the Relationship of the Church to Non-Christian Religions,* in *The Conciliar and Post Conciliar Documents of Vatican II,* ed. Austin Flannery, vol. 1 (New York: Costello Publishing Co., 1992) 738–42.

for it is there that the church can encounter the richness of modern culture and contribute to it as well as be influenced by it.

It was from Louvain University in Belgium and other European institutions having strong theological faculties, as well as a full range of other disciplines, that much of the theology which found its way into the documents of Vatican II came. In our rapidly changing world marked by an explosion of knowledge, there needs to be a lively dialogue between the various disciplines and the gospel. *Ex Corde Ecclesiae* lists "a continuing reflection in the light of the Catholic faith upon the growing treasury of human knowledge . . ."[7] as an essential characteristic of a Catholic university.

Theological research is a proper, and even necessary, activity for a graduate school of theology. Its findings, when sufficiently tested, become widely disseminated. One place where such learning should be shared is seminaries. A seminary offers professional education and formation programs. Its professional education is similar to that of a law school, that is, intended to prepare one for practice, for application, not for theoretical research, and its graduates are prepared for pastoral work. Yet seminary education should be in lively contact with theological research. Both need to be in dialogue with a wide range of other disciplines as they advance their fields of knowledge: while a seminary profits by association with a university and its theology faculty, it can be one of the places where theological investigation and research are tested for pastoral application. The faculty of the postgraduate seminary combined with that of the university's department of theology give St. Thomas a great theological resource and, therefore, the capability of a rich encounter of theology with modern culture.

A major constituent of St. Thomas is the local Catholic community which it serves in many ways, but none more important than the education of candidates for the priesthood. St. Thomas has two seminaries and is probably the only Catholic university in the United States having both undergraduate and postgraduate seminaries. There is evidence that it is a healthy situation for seminaries to be involved in university life and yet have the kind of environment that is conducive to spiritual formation and religious contemplation.

Seminary education is much more than the acquiring of a knowledge of theology; it also involves the acquiring of the skills and virtues that are expected to be found in a priest. The combining of a rigorous

---

[7] *Ex Corde Ecclesiae, Origins* 20 (4 October 1990) par. 1, A, 13.

theological education with an equally rigorous religious formation challenges St. Thomas. It has tried to meet this challenge by concentrating on theological instruction, because education is its proper role, and by leaving to others the formation programs while at the same time recognizing the need for close collaboration between the two. The formation programs are carried on at separate institutions on adjoining campuses which have residential facilities and chapels. They are staffed by professionally trained counselors and spiritual directors, all of whom have also had a solid theological education.

One can see that the opportunities for outreach and service are almost without number, limited only by initiative, creativity, and leadership. Leadership is of key importance and can come from many sources, but it usually requires cooperation from several university or university-related participants. In the cases cited in this chapter, leadership came from faculty, board members, students, off-campus friends, and the president. Not all of them participated in each project or to the same degree, but the general environment was one of openness to new initiatives and cooperation.

6

Service to the Catholic Community

A Catholic university has a primary responsibility to its students, to the general community of which it is a part, and also to the Catholic community from which it developed and continues to be nourished. Here two elements of its mission come together in important ways, namely, its mission of service and of religious commitment.

One of the great needs of the Catholic community in the past thirty years has been the religious education of all its young people. St. Thomas has been concerned about the church's school system, from kindergarten through high school, and about the religious education of all Catholic children. With the decline in the number of nuns, brothers, and priests who formerly staffed Catholic schools and with the continuing desire of Catholics to provide a Catholic education for their children, there has developed a great shortage of people with adequate religious knowledge to teach religion, with the result that sometimes the quality of religious instruction is inferior.

To remedy this situation, St. Thomas instituted a master's degree in pastoral studies as well as several noncredit programs. These are very helpful in preparing teachers of religious education in both school and nonschool circumstances, but they do not solve all the problems. Catholic schools need teachers who are well prepared to teach the various subjects commonly taught in schools and at the same time are knowledgeable in what constitutes a private religious school. For example, leadership in a private school does not require detailed knowledge of how public education is funded and relates to government agencies, but knowledge of how to fund and administer private education is necessary. To respond to these needs the university established within its school of education a division for private schools in order to help both administrators and teachers. It also set up within the undergraduate college an elementary teacher program. For many years students took their training in elementary teaching at the neighboring College of St. Catherine, but when the number of students became a burden to St. Catherine's, St. Thomas started a program on its own campus.

In the United States there are 11.8 million Catholics between the ages of five and seventeen. Of these, 2,252,450 attend Catholic schools. It is estimated that about the same number attend religious education classes for about one hour per week, thirty-four weeks a year, which are frequently taught by volunteers. But there remain 7,297,100, or about sixty-two percent, who are not receiving any formal religious instruction—an amazing number![1]

Obviously, this creates a great challenge for Catholic universities, a twofold challenge: how to assist parents and pastors in providing religious education and how to educate students in theology. Students arrive at the university who identify themselves as Catholic and yet are almost religiously illiterate. The preparation for courses in theology that formerly could be presumed no longer exists. Success in the endeavor at the kindergarten through high school level would mean that students coming to a Catholic university would be more able to profit from the religious education the university offers and that more students who appreciate their religion might choose to enroll in a Catholic college or university. However, the greatest beneficiaries would be the students, their parents, and parishes, which have the primary responsibility for religious education.

In an effort to meet this problem, St. Thomas established in 1975 the Center for Religious Education, which prepares lay people and religious to conduct religious education programs. It offers a master's degree program as well as short courses, workshops, and similar noncredit courses for those who need preparation for the teaching of religion. As a result of a needs assessment and in response to many requests, the offerings expanded to include liturgy, youth ministry, pastoral care, social justice, ministry to the mentally and physically challenged, and general adult religious education. In 1981 a Clinical Pastoral Education (CPE) program and other programs were instituted. By the tenth anniversary in 1985, the center had reached more than fifty thousand people.

[1] *Current Issues in Catholic Higher Education* 14 (summer 1993) 3–4.

In recent years the continuing education programs were reduced because of the development of duplicative programs by the Archdiocese of Saint Paul and Minneapolis and by the College of St. Catherine, although the university continues to provide a variety of courses. In addition, the department of theology offers continuing education courses in theology to teachers in Catholic schools. St. Thomas had responded to a need; eventually others followed its example. And there has been a similar history in areas of adult and continuing education in secular fields, the most notable example being in graduate business and management education where several institutions followed the university and initiated graduate programs.

St. Thomas has a modest endowment for financial aid to persons teaching in Catholic schools. In order to get the maximum benefit from these funds, the university decided to use them in a nontraditional way: a cohort system was introduced, with approximately thirty people constituting a cohort or class. By keeping a class together for at least most of their courses, optimum class size is maintained and, consequently, there is an economy of scale. There are also educational benefits from the exchange of experiences that come about as acquaintances and friendships, which might not take place if the students were broadly scattered, develop among the members of a cohort. The bonds that grow during the three-year period they are together prove helpful and supportive over the years.

The program is made available tuition-free to teachers and administrators in schools of the Archdiocese of Saint Paul and Minneapolis; the archdiocesan school system nominates a pool of candidates from which the university selects its students. Teachers must have been in the Catholic school system for three years and agree to remain in it for three years after receiving their master's degree. (Some go on for the educational specialist degree and the doctorate.) Endowment funds of the university cover some of the costs; the remaining costs are borne by the general funds of the university. St. Thomas' goal is to raise sufficient endowment funds to make it possible for every teacher, administrator, and counselor in Catholic schools to receive a master's degree. A unique feature of the graduate programs is that each student must take three theology courses, which as a rule are not required for graduate degrees, except of course those required for a degree in theology. This program is already being studied by other universities as a model. Its impact on the quality of education, especially its religious dimension, and on teachers' morale is enormous.

But St. Thomas has a more primary responsibility: to provide excellent courses in theology for its undergraduate students. It sees theology as an integral part of a person's education. Consequently, three courses or twelve hours of theology are required for the bachelor's degree. That is more than most Catholic colleges require, many of which cut back on the number of mandated courses during the period of great student unrest in the late 1960s and 70s. Having given up much of theology's place in the core curriculum, they have been unable or unwilling to reclaim the lost ground.

Theology and Christian philosophy are at the core of the Christian intellectual tradition. These programs must be related to the other disciplines, and that is perhaps the greatest academic challenge a Catholic university faces, given the departmentalization that has become a standard in higher education and given the secularization of many graduate schools. A department's hiring at least some persons who are knowledgeable in the Catholic intellectual tradition and can help their colleagues better understand that tradition is an excellent approach. Faculty development programs can also do much to remedy their deficiency in theological preparation, and summer workshops can be helpful, while sabbaticals for research in the religious and philosophical dimensions of a discipline are an additional means.

Campus ministry has a key role in relating theological studies to people's lives: it is "a constitutive element of a Catholic university,"[2] providing pastoral services, especially Mass, the sacraments, and preaching, as well as pastoral counseling and other services. However, it must go beyond these activities; it must help Catholics, both students and others, to integrate Catholic teaching into their lives so that it moves from intellect to will, from head to heart. Then faith is not only informed, it is alive. Homilies at Mass are an obvious way, and instruction which is directed toward faith development is another means of bringing religion and life together. Another way of helping students to live their faith is to foster outreach or service programs, such as working in kitchens that feed the poor, teaching the mentally challenged, finding shelter for and helping the homeless and assisting many others in need. Service in overseas missions is another learning and formative experience. All of this requires a director of ministry who is aware of new trends in theological studies so that material taught in theology classes can become the basis

---

[2] John Paul II, Pope, *Apostolic Constitution* Ex Corde Ecclesiae *of the Supreme Pontiff John Paul II on Catholic Universities*, Origins 20 (4 October 1990) par. 38.

of the faith formation of students. Above all, the director has to be a strong, self-reliant, self-directing, faith-filled person.

When one looks not just at the strictly intellectual tradition of the church but also at its broader cultural tradition, it becomes evident that the arts have an important position. This is true at all levels of education, even before formal schooling begins. The imagination of a child can be fired by pictures and music of Christmas, which are among the earliest learning experiences of most Christian children, by statues, paintings, crucifixes, Stations of the Cross. The image of Mary, the mother of Jesus, has a unique place in the cultural, theological, and imaginative tradition of the Christian church: a distinguished Lutheran scholar recently called attention to the unique role of Mary in Christian art down through the centuries.[3] She is the preeminent feminist who has uplifted the image and role of women from the ancient world to the present. Each era emphasizes different aspects of her life, and that is especially true in our age of feminism when a new assessment of her scriptural representation is taking place.

What does all this mean for a Catholic university? It at least means that the opportunity for courses in Catholic literature, art, and liturgical music should be taken advantage of; it means that a Catholic campus should be a congenial home for artists, writers, musicians, and others who carry on this living imaginative tradition. Such cultivation of creativity should be an integral part of a university education. It continues the education begun in early childhood, an education begun with religious experience before religious propositions were possible for the child. It rounds out the schooling of the student by adding an imaginative dimension to the purely intellectual, and thus the goal of educating the whole person is more fully realized.

Studies indicate that Catholic schools achieve the best results when they build layer upon layer, from kindergarten through grade school, high school, and college. It would seem likely that the accumulative process would be most effective when it included at all levels the development of the imagination as well as the intellect. Plays, concerts, Christmas and Holy Week pageants, religious art festivals, sculpture, trips to Rome, Florence, and other art centers, as well as courses in art and art history are some ways that the University of St. Thomas helps students develop their artistic creativity and appreciation. A unique and

---

[3] Jaroslav Pelikan, *Mary through the Centuries: Her Place in the History of Culture* (New Haven: Yale University Press, 1996).

instructive example of the arts at St. Thomas is the frescoes, the largest in the United States, on the ceiling and walls in the atrium of the main building on the Minneapolis campus. The artist, Mark Balma, working with students over two years, developed a renowned presentation of the seven virtues: faith, hope, charity, prudence, justice, temperance, and fortitude.

Andrew Greeley has pointed to the role of "the Catholic imaginative tradition" for Catholic education, including colleges.[4] In fact, he questions whether a college has a right to call itself Catholic if it does not include reflection on the church's imaginative heritage. William F. Lynch, S.J., has brought considerable scholarship to the role of the imagination in education.[5] In 1997 St. Thomas launched *Logos*, (a "Journal of Catholic Thought and Culture"); the theme of the first volume was imagination.

St. Thomas serves the Catholic community in still another way. It is a kind of service not usually associated with a university, for St. Thomas publishes the *Catholic Digest*. A mass market magazine, the *Catholic Digest* is not a medium of discourse among Catholic intellectuals; it is not a learned journal; neither is it a publication of opinion. It is intended for the ordinary reader and it endeavors to inspire, motivate, and inform about Catholic life. The Catholic Digest organization, wholly owned by the university, also operates the Catholic Digest Book Club, which each month recommends and makes available a book to the members of the club; approximately one hundred thousand are sold each year. In addition, it publishes a devotional magazine entitled *God's Word Today*, which informs people about sacred Scripture and provides a daily meditation on a biblical text.

This division of St. Thomas is clearly one of the most successful publication ventures in the church today. The *Catholic Digest*'s circulation of about four hundred thousand subscribers is the largest paid circulation of any Catholic magazine in the United States, probably twice the size of any other. Professional evaluation of its readership indicates that for every subscriber there are three other persons who read it. So its outreach to more than a million and a half people is impressive. Established in 1935 by three priests, the magazine's history reflects the experiences of the Catholic community through the Great Depression,

---

[4] Andrew Greeley, "The Catholic Imagination and the Catholic University," *Current Issues in Catholic Higher Education* 12, no. 1 (summer 1991) 36–40.

[5] See William F. Lynch, S.J., *Christ and Apollo: The Dimensions of the Literary Imagination* (New York: Sheed and Ward, 1960).

World War II, the anticommunism of the Cold War, the early years of the liturgical and civil rights movements, and the renewal of Vatican II. In gradual and sometimes subtle ways, it has played a part in the very life of the church for over six decades, and for more than half of that time it has been the property of St. Thomas.

Its success is due to many factors, among them the practice of always carefully surveying its readers, average men and women in the church pew on Sunday, to find out what their interests are. Those who want more intellectual depth have a wide range of Catholic magazines from which to choose. Such magazines have relatively small circulation while the *Catholic Digest* is edited for a mass market. Over the years the educational level of the Catholic population has risen and the magazine has moved accordingly, both leading and reflecting its readers. Several Catholic magazines after Vatican II lost many of their subscribers, and some went out of existence. The *Digest* successfully navigated the perilous waters of the council's aftermath and retained its readership as it has in other difficult times. When St. Thomas acquired the magazine, there was concern, especially among some of its staff, that the university would change it into a "high brow" publication, with disastrous results in circulation. That, of course, never happened.

Another important factor in the success of the Catholic Digest enterprise is the quality of its leadership. Over the years it has had a professional staff, and for the past thirty its publishers have had extensive experience in producing general interest magazines and have brought that knowledge to the leadership of the *Catholic Digest*. The editorial and business staffs have also been professionally led. An advisory board, made up largely of outsiders who are publishers and business leaders and functioning as a governing board chaired by the president of the university, is a key factor in the success of the enterprise. These people bring knowledge of the profession as well as business acumen and standards. Under their guidance the magazines and book club are semi-autonomous and not commingled with the administration of the university. This allows the measurements of the publishing industry to be applied. At the time the Catholic Digest organization was acquired by St. Thomas, it was in a precarious financial condition, and the board played an important role in divesting it of several unprofitable undertakings and establishing competent management. It became not only financially stable but also profitable and continues to reach millions of readers and thereby to perform valuable service to the Catholic community. Once again, leadership is the key to success.

No university which claims to be Catholic can fail to include in its mission service to the Catholic community. At the core of this service is the formation of the minds and hearts of its students in the Catholic intellectual and cultural tradition. Some of the ways in which this dimension of the mission can be accomplished have been suggested in this chapter. There are many more. But in all of them leadership is the key to realizing this aspect as well as all the others of a Catholic university's mission.

II. Leadership

7

The Context of Decision Making

A mission statement means little without leadership. To be effective, it has to be translated into actions, and that requires leadership. The kind and quality of leadership put flesh and blood on the bones of the mission statement. It can be a mostly dormant document on a shelf in the president's office, or it can be a live and growing instrument shaping and guiding the university. What is abundantly clear is that leadership, especially presidential leadership, necessarily qualifies the mission and the mission, in turn, conditions the president's leadership.

We will now look at how leadership translated a mission statement into actions, into actions that transformed a small college into a university. All three elements of the mission, namely, religion, community service, and liberal arts education, were brought into play.

It is instructive to look at the environment in which leadership was exercised. What was the historical context of the university? What were the positions of significant groups of faculty, administrators, students, and supporters? What was happening in society beyond the campus? Presidential leadership does not operate in a vacuum, but in a very intricate web of relationships: all legitimate voices must be listened to with respect and openness.

One can readily identify three strands that make up the cloth that is the University of St. Thomas. They are, first of all, the traditionalists who want the university to continue as they thought it existed decades earlier; this is an ever dwindling group. Second, there are those who feel called to defend the place of either the liberal arts or business education. Finally, there are those who are deeply concerned about the religious identity of the university. Obviously, simply looking at the recent history of the institution in light of these three categories is simplistic since they often overlap; for example, the traditionalists sometimes rally to the side of the liberal arts against business administration. Nonetheless, it is helpful to separate out these three currents in an effort to understand what took place in the twenty-five years or more being analyzed here.

The first group opposed changes and wanted St. Thomas to remain as it had been, as they imagined it had been. They wanted a small college, highly focused, mostly on liberal arts. The historical reality was that it had not always been a college of the humanities, sciences, and arts only. In the beginning in 1885, it included a seminary, a high school, and a college which had a department of business administration or "commerce" almost from the start and whose sciences were mostly biology and chemistry, geared to preparing students to enter medical schools. Several departments, especially history, philosophy, and political science, were slanted toward the practical study of law and clerical training. In fact, in the period between World War I and the Great Depression of the 1930s, it had a law school, a school of commerce, and a school of engineering, all of which became victims of the Depression and ceased to exist.

That experience, the demise of the professional schools and the great financial problems that ensued, was traumatic and led to the opinion that St. Thomas should restrict itself to liberal arts and science at the undergraduate level. However, that position overlooked the fact that the best liberal arts colleges had great endowments, endowments of a size that St. Thomas had no hope of attaining as long as it offered only an undergraduate program. Its primary constituent base was the children, grandchildren, or great-grandchildren of poor immigrants. And while these were rising on the socio-economic ladder, they had not attained a state of established wealth which afforded them the capability to give substantial sums to the college. It was only after St. Thomas moved into the larger community and provided services to it that its endowment grew rapidly. Even its alumni and closest friends came to its support more generously when it provided more evident services to the community and the church. If one looks at the historical development of Catholic institutions in large urban areas, it becomes evident that many of them—those that became large and successful—responded to the educational needs of the communities in which they were located. In retrospect, it seemed almost natural that the University of St. Thomas should take the same path. The key was a readiness to be of greater service.

During the years that St. Thomas was undergoing its greatest changes, so was American society. In fact, society had entered a period of rapid change after World War II: the G.I. Bill for veterans of World War II made possible a college education for a whole generation of men who otherwise might not have gone to college; the Catholic population quickly became better educated and rose rapidly on the socio-economic ladder; and the need for adult continuing education also grew. So both a need and an opportunity existed, but by the 1980s tax-supported institutions in Minnesota, for a variety of reasons, were responding inadequately. St. Thomas and other private colleges stepped in and instituted new programs to meet the needs. This is a good example of the value of private or independent universities. A society as richly varied as the United States should have schools which have different kinds of programs and philosophies, serve different clientele and complement one another, and have the decision-making capacity to respond to needs and opportunities. More will be said later on how St. Thomas responded to a lack of educational opportunities, especially in business education, teacher preparation, and engineering.

During St. Thomas' transition from college to university, the opponents of change were but one element. More important was a built-in tension between those who saw themselves as defenders of the liberal arts and those who wanted a greater emphasis on more practical and career-oriented education. This tension was quite common in universities that had significant programs in business administration as well as in the liberal arts: put too simplistically, it was liberal arts versus business education. At St. Thomas, however, neither camp wanted to exclude the other. It was more a question of balance. The defenders of the liberal arts feared that business was becoming too large, too influential, and in danger of becoming predominant; some feared the university might be primarily seen as a business school.

There was some basis for this concern. As the university developed its professional programs at the graduate level, it came to the attention of many people who had not known it or paid attention to it. Approximately ninety-five percent of its students in its largest and best-known new program, the MBA, had not attended St. Thomas previously; they and their friends came to know the university because of its educational courses in business. Hence, in their image of the university, business loomed large. The irony of this was that the liberal arts were strengthened considerably as St. Thomas grew and improved financially because of the economies of scale and the new sources of revenue.

But, in fact, the tension between the two groups was healthy and it never pertained to fundamentals; neither wanted the other to be put out of the university. Those in the liberal arts wanted a sort of primacy: they wanted to keep business administration and wanted the students who majored in it to take the same core curriculum in a wide variety of disciplines as did students in other fields, but they became anxious when business became the largest department and was no longer one department among many. At the same time, its many students filled the classes in the core courses and thereby provided students for courses which otherwise might have small enrollments. The faculty in business administration valued the liberal arts dimension of their students' education because it gave the latter an edge over their competitors in many business schools. It was indeed a question of balance. Where the balance was to be struck was frequently a subject of discussion and tension.

In the debate on establishing separate professional schools, there was an effort to join the undergraduate department of business administration with the graduate program in a school of business. The undergraduate faculty favored keeping both programs separate, with the former staying in the liberal arts college. Many universities have a school of business in which all business courses carrying credit are taught, whether undergraduate or graduate. The St. Thomas faculty was convinced that by keeping the department of business administration in the liberal arts college, it would insure that the students received a liberal arts education. The faculty had the opportunity to drop business from the main college but chose not to do so; they regarded it as a valuable part of the institution that should be retained in a lively relation with the other undergraduate disciplines. It was the conviction of most of the faculty that the association of liberal arts and business gave students the best of two worlds: the core curriculum provided an education in the liberal arts, provided a breadth of education, and helped to train the student in rigorous thinking; instruction in business prepared a student for a job and gave a more practical dimension to education.

This combination of education in the liberal arts and business or the professions is consistent with Jacques Maritain's view. He wrote that "liberal education will permeate the whole of education. In other words popular education must become liberal, and liberal education must become popular."[1] Here Maritain contradicts Mortimer Adler, who, following Aristotle's division into the free and slaves, into a leisure class and a working class, wrote, "The good life depends on labor but consists in leisure."[2] Maritain's view calls for an integration of liberal education and education to earn a living, between the liberal arts and professional training. This wedding of education in liberal arts and business management is also a characteristic of the graduate school of management, although in a more limited way. Unlike some programs, it does not require a degree in business administration or economics for admission. Education to prepare people to be managers, leaders, decision makers is best carried out in a liberal arts environment. The broader the educational base—the greater the number of factors that can be brought to bear in decision making—the better the quality of leadership will be.

An example of this concern to integrate the liberal arts with business is a program established with the Aspen Institute, whose course in the great books carries credit for the MBA degree at St. Thomas. Traditionally, the institute has held it in August at its center in Colorado for senior and other high-level executives; their offering the same course on the university campus as an integral part of an MBA program is unique. It challenges students to look at their interests in their business activities in terms of some perennial questions of humankind; as such, it adds meaning to their lives and gives a larger perspective to their studies. It is a highly successful program, both in terms of student interest and in educational value.

Another successful effort to acquaint students with enduring values is the teaching of business ethics in an introductory graduate course designed to acquaint them with the field of management. It also is part of a capstone course on business policies, given at the end of the degree studies. In between these two "bookends," ethics is integrated with other subjects where it is relevant. The David and Barbara Koch Endowed Chair in Business Ethics, occupied by a distinguished ethicist, provides leadership, especially for the faculty, in business ethics. It is clearly evident that business management at both the undergraduate and

---

[1] Jacques Maritain, *The Education of Man,* ed. Donald and Idella Gallagher (1951; reprint, New York: Doubleday, 1962) 150.

[2] Mortimer Adler, "Labor, Leisure and Liberal Education" (1951), in *Reforming Education: The Opening of the American Mind,* ed. Geraldine Van Dorn (New York: Collier Macmillan, 1988) 108.

graduate level is involved with the values and other concepts of liberal education.

As we have said, there is tension between business and other disciplines, but it is a creative tension that challenges all sides and it is expressed in a civil discourse. The result is healthy and moves the university to great achievements and improvements. One side challenges the other and the end result is that each improves. There is, however, a danger that one side will block the other and a stalemate (a sort of gridlock) will result, but that has never been the case at St. Thomas. It was prevented by the goodwill and civility of the participants in the dialogue. Moreover, the discussions took place in a dynamic, challenging, questing, and open environment. The governance structure gave opportunity for people to put forth their ideas, and the decision-making process, with its use of committees composed of representatives from the affected groups, gave people an effective voice.

It was clear that an open style of administration made people feel free to express their opinions, to propose new programs, for example, the master's in business administration and other graduate-degree programs. Another example of a major initiative was the decision to become coeducational. The vice president for administration wrote a paper on the advantages and disadvantages of coeducation, but the first public step toward coeducation occurred when a faculty member rose at a faculty meeting and proposed that a committee be appointed to study the possibility of admitting women. One role of the president was to manage the inevitable tension so that it was creative and not destructive, to keep the channels of communication open, to keep the administrative and governance structure flexible and responsive. Another was to encourage, to support, to give to the committee's work a sense of meaning and accomplishment, on occasion to check some ill-advised initiative, and to lead, sometimes directly, other times indirectly.

There is a third basic element, in addition to business and liberal arts, in the mix at St. Thomas and that is the Catholic character of the university. Traditionally it was taken for granted that it was a Catholic institution: its faculty, staff, and student body were almost all Catholic; the Archdiocese of Saint Paul and Minneapolis furnished many priests to teach and perform other duties and, from time to time, also gave grants to the university, usually to pay debts. There was no regular annual subsidy from the archdiocese during much of the history of the university and certainly not in the last fifty years. Since the Catholic identity was taken for granted, there was little discussion of what it means. There were, however, visiting lecturers on Catholic subjects and an occasional article written on a Catholic subject.

However, as the number of non-Catholics employed by the university increased until they constituted approximately one-half of the faculty and staff, questions began to arise: What does it mean to say a university is Catholic? This question was further complicated by the changes and divisions within the church. Is the theology the university espouses liberal or conservative? Modern Catholicism embraces a wide spectrum of religious convictions and practices; the church is a changing church. Moreover, since Vatican II there has been an ongoing dialogue within the church, including the Vatican itself, on what constitutes a Catholic university. All of this has resulted in a certain confusion, especially among non-Catholics.

There was the further question: What can be expected of non-Catholics while respecting their religious freedom? If all faculty are expected to further the mission of the university and if one element of the mission is its Catholic identity, how can non-Catholics in good conscience comply with that expectation? The answer, of course, lies in the requirements of good scholarship which should include the teaching of all aspects of a subject. And if religious considerations are applicable, any qualified teacher should be able to teach them. In many disciplines the religious or moral considerations are those that are common to most religions, for example, the dignity of the human person, human freedom, and responsibility. The acid test might deem to be in the teaching theology from the Catholic viewpoint. There is the problem of whether one who stands outside the area of study can grasp the subject as well as one who knows it from the inside. Can a non-Jew teach about Judaism as well as a Jew can?

While a religious problem may not have been real for the most part, it is surely understandable that there should have been a certain degree of confusion, misunderstanding, and anxiety, not just on the part of faculty who are not Catholic, but also on the part of Catholics. So in the mix of change versus tradition, liberal arts versus business education, there was the ongoing concern about religious identity. There was not so much opposition, with rare exceptions, to including theology in the curriculum as concern: What did it mean? How would it be taught? What is theology's proper place in the curriculum? How many courses should be required for a degree?

There was also a vague fear among a minority that somehow the religious character was gradually being diminished and would eventually vanish. The history of many universities that were originally church-related and became secular, for example, Harvard University, was cited. George Marsden in excellent scholarly books has carefully documented how this association was eliminated or rendered nominal.[3] All religion was removed from the curricula of most American universities, despite the fact that the American people are predominately Protestant. This was consciously done by decision makers in higher education and not by default. By the beginning of the twentieth century the leading private universities were secularized; their Protestant connections were, at best, marginalized to the status of extracurricular activities.

While Marsden presents a persuasive case that key leaders in education deliberately excluded religion, there may be another dimension to the loss of church affiliation and that is that many of the churches lost interest in higher education: they no longer spoke to the universities, no longer challenged them, no longer had anything to say to them; furthermore, their own creedal positions were no longer as firmly held as they had been. Beyond this was the fact that the universities appealed to a broad segment of society while the denominations appealed to a narrower one, and this had financial implications: Did the churches want to or could they even financially support universities that welcomed everyone?

This loss of church affiliation did not immediately affect Catholic universities to any extent. But indirectly and over a period of time they were affected. Increasingly their faculties were educated, especially at the graduate level, at prestigious secular universities, and it thus became difficult for them to hire individuals who knew the relation of their discipline to religious teaching. Nevertheless, the history of some Protestant colleges was pointed to as an example of what might happen to Catholic colleges—indeed, for some critics it was already happening.[4] They saw American culture as predominantly secular and constantly threatening to overwhelm the religious aspects of all education.

This concern was shared not only by some within the academy but also by a few very articulate people outside the university. The changes

---

[3] George M. Marsden, *The Soul of the American University: From Protestant Establishment to Established Nonbelief* (New York: Oxford University Press, 1994), and *The Outrageous Idea of Christian Scholarship* (New York: Oxford University Press, 1997).

[4] See James Tunstead Burtchaell, "The Decline and Fall of the Christian College," *First Things*, no. 12 (March 1991) 16–29; no. 13 (April 1991) 30–38. See also Burtchaell's monumental work, *The Dying of the Light* (Grand Rapids: Eerdmans, 1998).

in religious practices since Vatican II seemed to lend some credence to the concern. The old forms of religious practices such as frequent attendance at daily Mass, an annual religious retreat, once compulsory in some places, no longer held sway. Instead, there was more participation in the liturgy by those who attended, more voluntary service to the needy and disadvantaged, Christian activities practiced to a greater degree than was done formerly. Religious life did not mean exactly what it had meant to an earlier generation. Was it better or worse? There was no certain answer, but many opinions. The controversy extended beyond curriculum to the entire university in all its activities. In fact, for many outsiders, there was more concern about speakers, student activities, the presence of gays, and similar matters, than there was about the curriculum. These concerns exist across the Catholic higher education community and St. Thomas was not exempt from them.

The interest in the religious and moral commitments of the university was healthy. It made some people more aware of Catholic identity and spurred them on to take action. For example, the establishment of a Catholic studies program and of conferences on the meaning of Catholic identity was due, at least in part, to the discussions and controversies over Catholic identity; the concern over how religion might relate to various secular subjects meant a reexamination of these subjects and their resulting enrichment, for instance, by the study of the religious and scientific positions on the origin of life, especially human life.

All of the three strands forming the warp of the tapestry of St. Thomas—liberal arts, business, and religion—contributed to a dynamism on campus. It was undoubtedly true that for many faculty, staff, and trustees the motivation to grow, to undertake new ventures, at least some of which entailed considerable risks, like the establishment of new campuses, was not specifically Catholic and perhaps not even seen as religious. For some people the desire to do good, to build a better community, to help people were probably more prominent motives. Some wanted to give a stronger ethical dimension to business and the professions. To make a substantial contribution to the quality of life of many people, to empower young people, especially women and minorities, to improve their lives, were also strong motives. For some people, all of these were religious motives. For others, they were simply good human responses to human needs and to opportunities. In many ways these motives coincided with or reinforced or were but a different statement of the effort to bring religious values into the daily lives of people, into the marketplace. In any case, the discussions and consultations which went on for a long time were a good example of how persons of good will and different motives can work together for the betterment of people.

The rest of the chapters in this section and those in the section that follows will concentrate on leadership and decision making and on how these operated in a Catholic institution; both should be seen in the context of the positions enumerated above. Following the discussion on leadership there will be a study of how it activated St. Thomas' mission in a number of new programs.

8

Presidents Make a Difference

"Presidents Make a Difference" is the title and thesis of a report by the Commission on Strengthening Presidential Leadership. It insists on the central importance of presidential leadership saying, in part, "Colleges and universities are fragile and precious to society. Leadership of these institutions is important. . . ."[1] While there is no commonly accepted definition of leadership, in a general way it can be said leadership is the ability to set and articulate a direction or goals, then gain commitment to those goals and motivate people to achieve them. It is as much an art as a science because it deals with many variables and much uncertainty and requires intuition, judgment, and experience.

Having looked at some environmental factors that influenced the leadership and the decision-making process at St. Thomas, this presentation will now focus on the leadership that brought about the developments which took place in rapid succession. What was the vision, the motivation, the decision-making process, and the risks involved in the transformation of the institution? Considerable attention will be paid to the Catholic character of the institution because it constituted an essential part of both the vision and the motivation, certainly for the president as well as many others; in fact, it probably was a decisive element for most of the decision makers, even if they were not fully conscious of it.

---

[1] Commission on Strengthening Presidential Leadership, *Presidents Make a Difference* (Washington, D.C.: Association of Governing Boards of Universities and Colleges, 1984) 102.

Dr. Robert Terry, director of the Reflective Leadership Center of the Hubert H. Humphrey Institute of Public Affairs at the University of Minnesota, has written: "Leadership addresses the fundamental core of human life, focusing on issues of courage, vision, ethics and spirituality, as they contribute to the definition of, and action toward, the common good. Thus leadership is less a series of skills than a profound mode of engagement in the world."[2] If leadership involves the "fundamental core of human life" and "spirituality," then one would expect that at a Catholic institution Catholicism would influence leadership. To leave this element out would be misleading and a distortion; on the other hand, to make it all pervasive and determinative would be unrealistic.

Terry's observation is profoundly true, especially in regard to academic leadership: the character of leaders will reveal itself. People who devote their lives to a university are seldom motivated primarily by money; financial incentives loom larger in business than in academia. Academicians are largely motivated by their love of their subject matter and by a desire to accomplish something that truly benefits others. They expect their colleagues to be people of integrity and ideals; they especially expect to find these qualities in people who have positions of leadership.

In higher education, leadership is different from what it is in business. It is scattered among governing boards, administrators, faculty, students, alumni, friends, and sources of funding, whether public or private. The president has only limited authority over faculty and students and even less over the other groups. Obviously, a high premium must be placed on cooperation. This, in turn, requires on the part of leadership trust, confidence, consistent and persistent performance. Leaders who are seen as hardworking, fair, and cooperative and have a good "track record" of success will have the trust of their various constituencies. Such leaders will also have their confidence since they have been successful in past endeavors and there is a presumption that they will be successful in current and new proposals. It is clear that academic leadership involves fundamental character traits, such as evenhandedness, justice, candor, openness, and ultimately one's treatment of people. Successful leaders generally possess these qualities, at least in some measure. All of these qualities are related to religious virtues or values. This brings one back to Terry's position that leadership is based on a

---

[2] Robert Terry, "Intuitive Leadership: A Research Project of the Reflective Leadership Center," Hubert H. Humphrey Institute of Public Affairs (Minneapolis: University of Minnesota Press, 1988) 2.

vision of life, ethics, and spirituality. In the case of the University of St. Thomas, that vision is Catholic, hence, this study treats its religious, specifically Catholic, commitment at length.

However, academic leadership cannot be capsulated by a general reference to the fundamentals of character. Many specific traits, besides those already listed, are also important, among them industriousness. Willingness and the ability to work hard are prerequisites for a successful presidency—one who is not willing to take on an unrelenting round of duties should not be president of a university. The demands of the job also require sacrifices of personal interests; family and social involvements can suffer. It is said that many persons who have a close-up view of the job of president today, for example, vice presidents and deans, increasingly refuse to be candidates for a university presidency because of the burdens of the office.[3] Nevertheless, a range of benefits flows from the commitment to hard work, enhanced moral authority for instance. At a more practical level, there is increased effectiveness in doing the job because of frequent and wide contacts with people who have helpful information.

One of the myths about leadership is that successful leaders are somewhat remote, have a hands-off relationship to their university, and spend their time in abstract reflection and planning for the institution. They have few, if any, regular duties and extensively delegate tasks to others so that they need not be involved in the day-by-day activities. J. Henry Mintzberg of McGill University says this image is false: "Study after study has shown that managers work at an unrelenting pace, that their activities are characterized by brevity, variety, and discontinuity, and that they are strongly oriented to action and dislike reflective activities."[4] He speaks of the manager's job as enormously complicated and difficult. What is true of managers in business is also true of their counterparts in academia. If they and their universities are to be successful, they must be willing to work very hard.

Willingness to work diligently, if extended over a long period, gives experience, and experience is often the basis of what is known as intuition. Experience and intuition are constitutive of good decision making

---

[3] For a study of effective presidents as contrasted with average college presidents, see James L. Fisher and others, *The Effective College President* (New York: MacMillan and American Council on Education, 1988).

[4] Henry Mintzberg, "The Manager's Job: Folklore And Fact," *Harvard Business Review* (March–April 1990) 164.

and leadership. Jay A. Conger cites two extensive studies of successful leaders which found that "experience was a common denominator in the ability of all these individuals to lead. . . ."[5] But gaining experience takes time—an argument for long tenure if the incumbent leader is successful.

Planning is another important part of leadership. The entrepreneurial academic president, however, sees the limited value of a classic long-range plan with its statement of mission, goals, objectives, and timetables. It does serve as a tool to guide conversation about and understanding of the institution; it helps in defining responsibilities and procedures for the day-by-day work of the institution in ways that optimize resources, and if the process of making the long-range plan involves the entire academic community, helps people think about the mission and character of the institution and how these relate to the ongoing activities. In this way the process helps to develop consensus on many matters, and the long-range plan becomes imbedded in the thinking of people and even subconsciously influences their behavior.

However, because the opportunities that move a university ahead are often outside the plan, the effective president has the ability, the freedom, and the initiative to seize such an opportunity. This does not mean a disregard of the plan, but rather an understanding of its limits. The president needs the freedom to innovate. An institution small enough for the president to be close to its leaders and influence them directly does not need the rigidity and uniformity that a larger institution needs and that a master plan can give. The president then has the freedom to look for new or better ways the institution can attain its goals and can innovate and implement new ideas. But to be innovative, presidents must have some discretionary funds so that they can experiment and move quickly when windows of opportunity open up. This was certainly the case at St. Thomas during its years of fast growth.

Robert Peck, after studying nineteen successful colleges chosen out of a group of two hundred, concluded: "The small independent college is an entrepreneurial enterprise and its leaders are entrepreneurs in the best classical sense. Just as the concept of entrepreneurship is necessary to understand the development of economic systems, so it is required to comprehend the development of the American education system."[6]

---

[5] Jay A. Conger, *Learning to Lead* (San Francisco: Jossey-Bass, 1992) 29.

[6] Robert A. Peck, "The Entrepreneurial College Presidency," *Educational Journal* (winter 1983) 18–25.

One does not ordinarily look for entrepreneurship in university administration. Leadership in educational institutions has traditionally been conservative, cautious, and willing to take few risks. There are many reasons for this, including the personality profile of many persons attached to academic life. They place a high premium on security and predictability, while entrepreneurial leadership involves prudent risk-taking and a willingness and capability to grasp opportunities when they arise. At St. Thomas an evolving mission and a new kind of leadership gave a dynamic quality to the institution, which grew in size and changed in service. There is considerable difference between maintaining or managing an existing university and creating a new university or new life for an existing institution. Both require excellent management and the handling of problems. New institutions, however, call for creativity, risk-taking, and entrepreneurship. These are qualities of a quite different character.

Successful presidents combine administration and entrepreneurship. They plan from the left side of the brain and manage from the right.[7] In routine matters they are good administrators; in dealing with problems, uncertainty, and ambiguity, they are entrepreneurs—risk takers; in decision making, they rely heavily on experience and intuitive judgment. Neither intuition nor experience is a substitute for hard work, for data collecting, for listening carefully to a wide range of opinions, but in the end the decision maker arrives at a judgment that is personal and may seem to be subjective. The responsibility for the decision and its consequences can drive the considerations to a great depth in the decision maker's consciousness, in the person's very being, that is not understood by those who are less involved. When the moment of decision is reached, the decision maker has a feeling of confidence, certainty, and satisfaction which others who have not gone through the process do not experience. It is a creative moment and to observers may sometimes seem to be lacking in objectivity, perhaps even arbitrary. Only its successful outcome will demonstrate its reasonableness.

The successful president creates an environment, an openness that encourages people to set forth their ideas. Here is an illustration: the University of St. Thomas had long-range plans for more than twenty years, during the time when its greatest development was taking place. Yet this did not flow directly out of the plans; it came about by identifying needs and creating solutions to them, and the source of an idea could be anyone. For example, the idea of a graduate program in business,

---

[7] Mintzberg, "Manager's Job," *Harvard Business Review* (July–August 1976) 57.

the MBA, came from the chairperson of the undergraduate department of business administration; a faculty member, with credentials in both business and engineering, for several years championed the establishment of a program in engineering, and when it was founded, he became its chairperson.

Because of the importance of intuition and judgment, it may seem to some that the president uses plans and consultations only as window dressing—they fail to understand the nature of entrepreneurship and its role in the governance of independent institutions. Likewise, the process of consultation, the time it takes, the many constituencies whose opinions might be solicited may seem to indicate the president is indecisive, whereas the reality may be that he/she is gathering information, learning, and taking the time necessary to assimilate the information.

Mintzberg observes that an institution, to be creative, must "rely largely on one individual to conceptualize its strategy, to synthesize a 'vision.' . . ." He continues, "Scratch an interesting strategy, and you will probably find a single strategy formulator beneath it. Creative, integrated strategies seem to be the product of single brains. . . ."[8] A problem for the "single strategy formulator" is that his/her "vision" is often never complete. It is not fully worked out in advance as the decision maker moves by incremental steps. He/she may not know where things will finally end. One step leads to another. Gradually the picture, the vision, becomes clearer. No one in the group or academic community may know in advance what the possibilities are. The end of the road cannot be seen; it is enough to see the next step. Ultimately the end of the road comes into view.

This was certainly true of the recent developments at St. Thomas. For example, the MBA began with a program to educate generalists in business (managers) and gradually moved into various concentrations from marketing to accounting and nonprofit organizations. The success in business education at the graduate level encouraged other departments to develop their own graduate programs, as in social work and English literature. One successful undertaking led to another, and it gradually became clear that St. Thomas could, and should, become a comprehensive teaching university. The concept of such a university was itself an evolving one. The needs of society call for institutions whose research would be more application oriented than theoretical, which embraced many fields of endeavor and learning. An institution

---

[8] Ibid., 56–57.

that responds to a wide range of needs, including applied research, and has good teaching as its highest priority becomes a new kind of university, even if the vision of its full potential has not yet completely evolved.

People who want a fully formulated plan before action is taken can become dissatisfied in such an environment. Sometimes, even if one wants to complete a strategic plan, it is impossible to do so and to adhere rigidly to it. Opportunities arise; they are fleeting and must be seized or they are lost. When a university becomes known for its openness to new ideas and for creativity, many proposals come to it. Some of them fit the mission and the resources and must be adopted as soon as possible or the opportunity will be lost. An example of leadership in such circumstances is the classroom-faculty office building on the university's St. Paul campus. It is known as the O'Shaughnessy Educational Center and was built in 1969. Before then the federal government had a program of grants for academic facilities, but St. Thomas did not meet the criteria for these when the program began. But by 1968 it did and received a grant which had to be matched by private donations. Some faculty members strongly objected to constructing a badly needed building because they wanted the fund-raising efforts directed to increasing faculty salaries. Nonetheless, the grant was accepted, additional money raised, and the building constructed. Very shortly afterwards federal funding stopped: if the building had been delayed, there would have been no funds and no building. An opportunity appeared for a very short time. Decisive action was clearly in the best interest of the university.

The venturesome and timely character of decision making can be a fertile ground for complaints from friends and foes alike because they feel they are not adequately consulted. In a dynamic institution, events sometimes outrun communication because of the nature of the opportunity and because the decision maker may carry in his/her head a vision or a plan that he/she has not had time to articulate to those who think they should be consulted or informed in advance. This can lead to criticism, especially if intuitive decisions happen frequently or if they seem impulsive rather than based on sound judgment. This, in turn, opens up questions of the track record of the leader and the relationship with constituents. This is particularly true when critics do not really understand planning and how decisions are made and how a private institution must act if it is to progress.

The incremental development of a vision can also be a source of misunderstanding, especially with those whose idea of planning is that of the classic long-range plan that is "objective," deduced from certain principles and assumptions, static and rigid, the kind that fits large organizations. In large universities and systems of higher education, managerial ability, the ability to follow the classic pattern of management, may be important. The classic vision or master plan is helpful in large businesses, in the military and government, and in large educational systems. It works best in conditions of predictability, stability, and an underlying understanding that things will go on much as they have been. However, the master plan becomes restrictive if people rigidly adhere to it: opportunities that were not foreseen when the plan was made are passed by because they don't fit into it.

For several years St. Thomas engaged in long-range planning according to the classic model, trying to follow those used in big business and the other large organizations which were then held up as the standard. The federal government and foundations encouraged such exercises; for example, in the early 1960s the Ford Foundation urged universities to follow the Tickton model of planning, and while the process was of some help, it never seemed to fit what really took place. The static view of a university that prevailed in such plans led to discouragement. It was Peck's study of the most successful small colleges that opened up a new vision or understanding of how excellent small colleges really worked and how their leaders functioned.

The conflict between the classic plan and the entrepreneurial plan of development is illustrated by problems St. Thomas had with neighborhood organizations which constantly wanted a detailed plan for the physical development of the institution, a map of where new buildings would be located and when. They were accustomed to dealing with government planning; however, private nonprofit institutions, unlike state units that have dependable tax support, can build only when donors are available, and donors' preferences vary so that it is not always possible to say what buildings will be built and when they will be built. The best that can be done is to prepare a very tentative plan. Unhappily, it is often so tentative it creates as many problems as it addresses as far as the rigid planners and critics are concerned.

It was incumbent upon the leadership of the university to try to understand the position of the property owners: their pride in their neighborhood, their sense of security, their emotions, their financial interests. This calls for frequent and open communication and a willingness to compromise. In the decade of the 1980s, St. Thomas agreed not to acquire property on three sides of its campus, and in return, the community organization agreed not to oppose an extension of the zoning area on the university's south side which would permit the joining of its two campuses. There were other accommodations on both sides, and the normal fears of some people that the changes would have a deleterious effect of the neighborhood proved to be groundless. A new era of friendly cooperation developed.

Trust in a leader is the product of a leader's character, hard work, experience, and achievement. It is the most essential element of leadership. People will follow a leader whom they trust and know to be successful. Even when they question a proposal or course of action, their trust in their leader allays their doubts. The following chapters should be read in the light of entrepreneurial leadership as well as a particular philosophical/theological stance.

9

Leadership and Core Values

Much of the literature on presidential leadership speaks about a grand vision of what an institution can become. It includes major plans for development and improvement. It sums up the hopes and aspirations and dreams with enough specificity to give an aura of attainment. In the instance of the University of St. Thomas, that was not the situation. The president did not come to the office of president with a grand vision or master plan that would guide him during his tenure. Rather, he accepted the general direction the institution was going, that is, as a fairly typical liberal arts college. He did, however, have a strong conviction that education should be value oriented and have a clear connection with one's daily life: the classroom and the community need to be related; religious values and principles should be taught and then brought to bear in the community. This conviction was more fundamental than any long-range plan could be, for it was grounded in a stance toward life. It both grounded and motivated presidential leadership and thus became a lived reality that gave great vitality to the mission.

A community needs leaders who are well educated in areas that relate to the quality of life in a community and have strong ethical and religious values, who see their business/professional life and all other aspects of life as a related whole and who are dedicated to the good of a community. Among such areas are education, communications, technology, religion, and business. St. Thomas ventured into academic programs related to these fields.

In these and other areas a university can have a significant role in determining the quality of life in its community. But to do so, leadership is required, a leadership that today is holistic and aware of opportunities, that flows from a vision which sees all life as a seamless cloth and from a readiness to seize opportunities. There is no shortage of good ideas or of people to propose them. It's the role of a university president to encourage people to think of ways of doing their job better and to be willing to present their ideas; then to sift through their proposals, to test those that seem to fit the institution, its mission and resources; and then to act upon those that are most promising.

The needs of many communities are almost unlimited: change is certainly one of the main characteristics of our society, which needs people who can lead effectively and a work force trained to take advantage of the change. The logical place to provide such education is a university. There is, therefore, an unfolding range of opportunities for a university to be of service. What is needed is the will to grasp the opportunities.

Leadership is multifaceted. One success builds on another, and success builds confidence within the decision makers and in their followers. It is a common experience of successful leaders that the longer they have been in office and the more successful they have been, the greater the likelihood that they will get the necessary cooperation from others, even reluctant people, that is needed for success. The president must also believe strongly in the values at the heart of the university, the values that members of the academic community hold in common, and be able to articulate them and relate them to many different circumstances and programs. When new programs or new directions are undertaken, they must be related to the core values of the institution; then everyone can relate to the new endeavor.

It is necessary that faculty share the values of the institution. Hence, in hiring faculty, not only their expertise in the academic field must be taken into consideration, but their basic philosophy or orientation toward life must also be taken into account. This is particularly crucial for private universities because their distinctiveness is vital to their success and to the pluralistic enrichment and vitality of American higher education. These universities must hire people whose values are consistent with those of the institution and then provide a good program of faculty orientation. Only then can faculty members be expected to understand the character of the institution and contribute to its mission. In a well-governed university, the faculty has tremendous influence, in formal and informal ways, and if professors are expected to enhance not just their discipline but the whole university, they must be given the opportunity to understand clearly the history, tradition, values, culture, and broader environment of the university.

If a person's values are fundamentally inconsistent with those of the university, if a "fit" is not there, then both the individual and the university will suffer if the applicant is hired. Consequently, it is incumbent on both parties to be open and frank in stating their positions from the very first interview. Certainly in the case of a church-related institution religion is among the areas to be discussed. It is not necessary for every person to be of the same persuasion or denomination as the institution, but there should be understanding and respect: this is the minimum and a significant number in the faculty should be capable of championing the religious dimension of the university's mission if its distinctiveness is to be accentuated.

In an age that prizes programs insuring ethnic diversity and multiculturalism, such programs, valuable as they are, make it difficult to insist on fundamental and distinctive values. Government bureaucrats sometimes have a hard time understanding the intangible character of an institution; often they were educated in secular universities and have little or no understanding of value-oriented education. Many of them reluctantly allow consideration to be given to a teacher's values in the department or school of theology, but find it difficult to consider values in other disciplines. Yet it is precisely in disciplines premised on values or on a philosophy that the church-related institution can make a great contribution to the disciplines, to students, and to society. There is, therefore, a constant threat to the identity and distinctive effectiveness of these institutions; if that identity is lost, the end result could be a colorless, nondescript education. The very pluralism that has so enriched American culture would be denied one of its constitutive elements in the name of equal opportunity, diversity, nondiscrimination, objectivity, and value neutrality. These values (except value neutrality) are important and can be achieved without threatening religious distinctiveness; in fact, much of their strength and attractiveness is based on religious and moral values. In the long run survival depends in a considerable measure on their moral and religious underpinning. Equality and fairness have a natural ally in religion and morality. They should not be placed in opposition in hiring practices.

It is clear that if the core values of a university are not shared by both the president and the faculty, then the ability of the president to lead is endangered. It is the core values by which the desirability of new ventures is tested; at the same time the conviction that the values deserve to be more widely shared drives the institution to consider new ventures. The president has the task of finding a balance between holding firmly to the traditional and fundamental values of the institution and maintaining an openness to change. In the case of St. Thomas, liberal arts education has been a basic commitment from the beginning. As more and more business-related programs were proposed, their liberal arts values had to be accentuated so that business education fit comfortably with liberal arts values in both the undergraduate and graduate programs. The role of the president was to hold fast to institutional commitments while welcoming new developments.

The president must have the ability to seize opportunities when they become available. This implies the freedom to make decisions and to act. If the academic bureaucracy is too cumbersome and slow, if the academic community is divided, the president may have little opportunity to exercise initiative. Frequently the presidents of private institutions are better able to move more quickly and decisively than their colleagues in state universities where the bureaucracy is more entrenched and multi-layered. The governing board of a state university is more likely to have a watchdog mentality toward the president and the institution because public funds are used, while at a private university the governing board is more likely to be supportive of the president and to understand better the role of a chief executive.[1]

Much depends on the support the president receives from the governing board. One of the major assets of private education is its ability to innovate, to experiment, to act quickly to meet needs, and to relate to the community. The high competitiveness of the American economy enables successful business leaders to understand the importance of presidential leadership and to support it. They also understand the needs of the community, that is, the marketplace, and therefore are willing to respond to newly identified academic needs. And they recognize that service to a community in ways consistent with the character of the university adds to the quality of life in that community and is a great contribution that an alert and competent academic leadership can provide.

[1] See "Confessions of a Public University Refugee," Association of Governing Boards, *Trusteeship* 4 (May–June 1996).

10

Many Lead, One Governs

A successful university requires leadership in all areas: faculty, administration, students, and governing board. For a private institution probably the most important of these groups in regard to leadership is the board. By law it has final responsibility. It hires and dismisses the presidents. Between these two decisions, it monitors their work, guides, advises, supports, shields them from unreasonable criticism, and encourages them.

Others may judge that there are more important groups than the board, and in certain circumstances that may be true. In a state-supported university, if the governing board is made up of political appointees, the board may not have as positive an effect on the university as does the board in an independent university. Frequently the board members of such an institution do not have the same leadership status in the communities and organizations that are most important to a university as do their counterparts in independent institutions. Some may see themselves as protectors of certain interests and as overseers of a very large institution; some may not understand thoroughly the role of the president. Consequently, the president may rely more heavily on support from some other group, such as the faculty. Certainly no president can be successful without the support of the faculty, but the board of trustees is more directly related to presidential leadership than any other group.

It is fundamental that there be a clear understanding on the part of all the constituents of the university of the difference between policy and administration. Where the line is drawn should be clear. The board is concerned with policy matters. Policies may be formulated and shaped in many parts of the university, but the most important policies must be approved by the board, as must the president's most important decisions.

There are two traditions in American higher education on governance, and they can be the sources of confusion and misunderstanding. One tradition reaches back to the great medieval universities as they evolved within the church and later became self-contained independent communities of scholars who ruled themselves. Some of the features of this tradition are found most clearly in the great historic universities of England and the rest of Europe. This concept of semi-autonomy and self-governance lives on in American faculties. For example, academic freedom, as it has come to be understood in the United States, and academic tenure are basic building blocks of faculty status and self-governance. An elaborate committee system has become an integral part of university governance, and faculty serve on almost all committees and expect that decisions will be made by committees, or at least only after the committees on which they sit have been heard.

The other tradition is based on the American corporate model with its hierarchical structure. Universities are chartered by the state, and the governing board is analogous to the board of directors in a business corporation. Governing boards, whether of public or private institutions, tend to follow this tradition: they see themselves as accountable for the institution. Indeed, some state laws hold trustees personally liable for institutional financial failures. In the board's view, the president is comparable to the CEO (chief executive officer) of a business and the comparisons between education and business continue at lower levels. However, there are in fact important differences. Presidents of universities must rely more on persuasion than do their counterparts in business. Faculty tenure and academic freedom are limits to their authority, as is faculty expectation to share in governance. The line between their authority and the prerogatives of the faculty is often unclear. Faculty authority is greatest in academic matters because of the special competency of faculty in this area. It is less in other areas, such as finances or physical construction. There are many areas of mixed responsibility. This very uncertainty can give rise to exaggerated expectations and consequent disappointment when the expectations cannot be fulfilled. Overlapping interests occur, for example, when some faculty judge their academic colleagues primarily on the basis of the latter's competency in their academic field; administrators may look at faculty members in relation to students and proficiency in teaching and to a university's mission.

An example of confusion that can arise due to overlapping of responsibilities occurred during a major review of the St. Thomas undergraduate curriculum. The board of trustees and the faculty both had a role to play. At the beginning, the board stated that it was opposed to any lessening of the number of courses in theology and philosophy required of all undergraduates. It saw this as a safeguard of the Catholic character of the university and regarded that safeguard as its responsibility. It said nothing about the content of the courses, which was entrusted to the faculty, but only about the number of courses. Some faculty resented this, saying that it was an infringement on their prerogatives and that, in any case, the board should not have acted at the beginning of the process but only after the faculty had completed its work. On the other side, the board thought it was fairer to make its mind known before the faculty had spent time and work on the revision; it was fearful that to step in at the last minute could result in an unpleasant confrontation. Some of the faculty were undoubtedly interested in reducing the requirements in theology and philosophy, some saw it as an opportunity to challenge the role and authority of the board; but for most it was probably not a matter of great concern because it did not affect their turf and therefore did not lessen the number of courses for graduation offered by their department.

In addition to these considerations, students today expect not only to be heard but to have a share in governance, even representation on governing boards. Alumni associations, too, want a voice and a vote in governing. And increasingly, special groups have expectations; for example, business groups may have certain services or help they want from the university's school of business. The success of the university depends on the cooperation of all these groups. No one of them, except the governing board, can lead the university, but the faculty and students have a sort of veto. United and serious opposition from either of them would certainly cause the president or the board to reconsider any action they might want to take. All must discharge their rightful role and work together cooperatively if the university is to succeed.

Presidents must consistently try to clarify for each group their responsibilities. They must interpret the constituencies to one another because the latter's cooperation and leadership in areas of their greatest competency are so very important. But for institution-wide leadership in a private university, the board must take the field. Consequently, the

relationship between the board and the president is of critical importance. A strong board gets a strong president; it will not be satisfied with
mediocre performance. A strong president will get a strong board. If the
board is not strong, such a president will work to change the composition of the board to make it strong, and the willingness of competent
people to serve on the board is frequently related to the degree of confidence the prospective member has in the president.

The board of trustees, or whatever name is given to the governing
body, holds an institution in trust, as this name implies. It has a basic responsibility to pass an institution on from generation to generation.
People commit their lives and their treasure to a university because they
believe in what the university represents, its values, its kind of education
and service, and the board has a sacred trust to guard the university's
integrity, its mission, and its resources. This is not a static function but a
dynamic one. In a rapidly changing society, the board must guide the
development of the institution; it must lead in positioning the university within the community and in relation to its constituents.

In a Catholic institution many, perhaps all trustees, whether Catholic or of other faiths, see its Catholic character as a fundamental and integral element of the university; all are committed to certain values that
have a religious base and are important for the development of character and of citizenship. The welfare of business and professions, vital to a
healthy community, depends on moral values. The root of such values
in a Catholic institution is its Catholicism. In the normal course of events
a Catholic institution's board will have a predominance of Catholics by
a process of natural selection. Many alumni are Catholic and, as alumni,
have a strong interest in the university and are willing to serve it. People
willing to give time, talent, and treasure, and to take on the responsibilities of leadership often have strong religious motivation; they believe
deeply in the religious mission of the institution. From such people
come those who make excellent, committed trustees.

In a church-related university certain positions on the governing
board are frequently reserved for representatives of the sponsoring denomination or religious body. This has several advantages, such as historic continuity, support from the sponsoring body, and identity. The
danger in this arrangement, in contrast to a totally self-perpetuating
method of selecting trustees, is that the representatives of the sponsoring body might not fit the needs of the board at a particular time. The
solution lies in proper balance: a board should be balanced with different kinds of talents, for while money is always important, there are

many people whose talents and experiences lead to careers which are not highly remunerative.

A board also brings to a university the viewpoints of outsiders. This is a stabilizing and positioning influence. It represents the broader public, not in the sense of the representation of special interests, which can be dangerous, but in the sense of the communities, both civil and religious, to whom the university owes allegiance. At St. Thomas three of the forty-three positions are ex officio. One is held by the archbishop of the Archdiocese of Saint Paul and Minneapolis, which is the sponsoring body. He is the chairperson of the board, the vicar general of the archdiocese is the vice-chair, and the president of the university holds the third position.

In October 1970 the president asked for an evaluation of his performance and that of the board of trustees. A committee studied the matter and in April 1971 reported that in its judgment the key question was the relationship of the board to the archdiocese. Board members frequently assumed that the archdiocese was financially responsible for the university. On the other hand, the archbishop regarded the board as responsible. Each side thought the other was the primary responsible agent. The result was a sort of stalemate. Things were left to the president and the administrative staff or were not done. The result of the discussion was that the board took more responsibility. It became more active, especially in financial affairs. It was recognized that the archdiocese does not have the resources to be the major source of financial help; its primary contribution was the services of the diocesan clergy, who were compensated at a level substantially below that of their lay colleagues. This was a turning point in the leadership roles of the university. The minutes of the board of trustees meeting on October 24, 1972, record the president and board discussing the budget in relation to admissions, student-faculty ratio, and tuition levels. Again, in an October 1973 meeting, the president discussed the budgetary implications of these same matters.

In 1973–74, gifts reached an all-time high and a new deferred-giving program was launched. It would be impossible to determine to what extent the increase in contributions was due to the clarification of responsibilities between the board of trustees and the archdiocese and to what extent it was due to new fund-raising programs. However, inasmuch as the archdiocese made no direct contribution either before or after the report by the committee, it would seem that the increase in contributions came about because of increased attention to fund-raising on the part of both the board and the administration.

The board reconsidered the role of the archbishop and concluded that he should continue as chair. Among the reasons for its decision was the enhancement of St. Thomas' relationship with the archdiocese: this arrangement has kept the archbishop involved in the life of the academic community, and his presence is a constant reminder to the board and others of the Catholic character of the university.

The role of a governing board within the institution seems to be directly related to the maturity of the university. Historically, in private institutions the first group to become professional and organized was the faculty, which thus acquired a central role in governance. In addition, presidents and deans frequently came out of the faculty and returned to it when they left administration. But, gradually, as administration in general became more complicated, schools of administration were established and administrators began to be professionally prepared for their tasks. For universities the result has been greater efficiency and better administrative leadership. In fact, quite apart from the question of greater efficiency, the growing complexity of university administration has necessitated the development of professionally competent administrators. Contact with universities that do not have trained administrators, for example, in some of the less-developed countries, shows how important professional administrators are to the life of a university.

Unfortunately, in some institutions the development of a professional class of administrators, some of whom have not had faculty experience, has contributed to a split between faculty and administrators that is antagonistic and therefore wasteful of energy and destructive of cooperation. Also, some faculty members feel that administrators who have not been teachers do not really understand the lot of the teacher. All of this may have contributed to the unionization of faculties that has taken place in recent years in some institutions.

Over time, boards became better organized, attracted greater talent, persons more experienced in leading large organizations. At the same time, the legal responsibilities and liabilities of board members became more evident. As boards became more conscious of their role and more active in the life of universities, both faculty and administrators sometimes felt that they were losing influence, that the boards were taking over areas of governance which belonged to them by tradition. Actually, the leadership of boards strengthened and improved the entire institution and everyone was better off.

In the 1960s there was considerable discussion in Catholic circles about the role of the board in a Catholic university. Boards had been predominantly composed of members of the sponsoring religious organization. In fact, the religious group frequently owned the university. Sometimes there was only one corporation for both the religious community and its schools. As the demands on private universities became greater, it was increasingly necessary to enroll the help of lay people; also, the Second Vatican Council (1962–65) called for greater lay leadership in the church. Lay people bring different perspectives to the deliberations of a board; they also reach out to many areas of the community. As Catholic colleges and universities moved more and more into the mainstream of American society, they needed the help of lay leaders. At the same time, it was difficult for the religious communities to give up exclusive governance of their property, built up over many years with great sacrifice on the part of their members.

This was not a problem for the University of St. Thomas. It had lay members on its governing board from the beginning, and the lay members were equal voting members, not second-class members serving in a merely advisory status. St. Thomas was probably the first Catholic university in the United States to have a predominantly lay board with full governing and financial responsibilities. Its history showed that the fear that a lay board would lead to secularization—as happened in some Protestant universities—was groundless: lay members are as committed to the Catholic identity as are the clergy. As long as persons are selected for the board on the solid principles of commitment to the mission of a university and "fit" its spirit, the board will continue to discharge its basic responsibility of holding the university in trust from generation to generation. In January 1967—before the movement toward lay boards was well under way—the president of the university addressed the First Friday Club (a distinguished lay group) in Washington, D.C., and related the St. Thomas experience and encouraged universities to move in the direction of lay boards.[1]

As needs arose, the St. Thomas board was enlarged, mostly with lay people, until today there are forty-three positions, five of which are held by priests and include the three ex officio positions. This composition gives a great variety of talent and access to many segments of the community. The stature of the board members in the community gives great credibility to the university and makes supporters confident that it is well managed. Such confidence is fundamental for raising funds.

[1] *College and University Newsletter,* 3 February 1967, National Catholic Educational Association, Washington, D.C.

Board members are in particularly good positions to lead in fund-raising. Their membership on a board is evidence to potential donors of their commitment, and they themselves often make substantial gifts. They have access to major decision makers in business, foundations, and government and can open doors that the president of the university cannot. Nevertheless, questions arise about the function and makeup of boards. Where do they get their information and is their composition skewed to favor certain interests, for example, conservatives or liberals? Both of these questions express legitimate concerns.

Members should be selected for a board on the basis of what talents and resources the board needs at any particular time: What can a prospective new member bring to the work of the board? In some public universities the selection of members to represent certain interests and areas may be workable. The danger is that in looking after the interests they represent, members may lose sight of the overall good of the institution. Thus, great care must be exercised to get people who are competent, fair-minded, who do not have special causes to advance, and who are committed to the goals of the university. Generally speaking, such persons are available for service at private universities, for there is little, if anything, the university can do to help them in their business or profession. Certainly the experience at St. Thomas is that no one has ever asked for special consideration. The board follows a hands-off policy in the selection of faculty and in the content of courses; hence, it does not interfere with the work of the classroom. While there is a preponderance of business executives, as would be expected, there are also people who bring to the board's deliberations their experience in labor, politics, education, community service, and the church.

Where does the board get its information about St. Thomas? A large number of board members are alumni, some are parents of students or recent students, many have friends who are associated with or interested in the university and are sources of information. Most members have had experience on committees and other boards and understand generally how boards work; for example, they know the difference between policy-making and administration, they know not to try to micro-manage the university.

The president of each university has a responsibility to acquaint new board members with its policies, practices, financial and physical condition. At St. Thomas, the board committees invite input from the various constituencies of the institution; for instance, the academic affairs committee meets with faculty members and the student affairs committee meets with students. Such direct input frees the committees from relying exclusively on administrators for information. Each committee is assisted by a staff person from the administration. Vice presidents attend board meetings and can be questioned directly by its members, and the alumni/ae elect a representative to the board. Board members seem satisfied with the sources and the amount of information they receive. A member once remarked: "I think I know a great deal about the institution and its operations. I wish I were more involved in the social life of the academic community." St. Thomas has a well-informed, knowledgeable, and unusually competent board of trustees.

Today it is difficult to think of a first-rate private university without the active leadership of its governing board. Certainly the history of the University of St. Thomas would have been greatly different if it had not had the leadership of a strong board of trustees.

What a marvelous institution the governing boards of private universities are! They are said to be uniquely American. Such boards bring together an array of talent that could not be hired, and unlike service on for-profit boards, there is no compensation. Just the opposite. Board members are often expected to contribute financially to the institution. Board membership can also consume a lot of the time of very busy persons. Clearly, members of these governing boards are very special people: they are motivated by a strong conviction of the worth of private education both for the individual and for the community.

Leadership is diffused throughout a good university. In the day-to-day operation, especially in academic matters, the faculty has a most important leadership role. At St. Thomas, until 1991, the faculty governed its deliberations and decision making by a rather traditional college organization which it had instituted. As the university grew, as the faculty increased in size, and especially as professional programs at the master's and doctorate levels increased, the faculty became increasingly uneasy with an organizational structure it had designed when the institution was a college.

After considerable study, the faculty, with the concurrence of the board, decided to change to a senate style of governance so that teachers at the undergraduate level would meet separately from those teaching graduate courses. This would allow those actually engaged in programs to make the decisions concerning them. The lines of authority and responsibility were clearer. A series of other decisions had to follow from this structural change, such as designating who were graduate faculty and who were undergraduate faculty as well as many procedural matters. The position taken by the administration was that this was largely a faculty matter and whether it ruled itself under a college plan or under a senate plan was for it to decide. The relationship of the president, academic vice president, and deans to the faculty bodies was important to the administration, and a satisfactory arrangement was worked out. The ease with which this new structure came into play was evidence of the excellent cooperation which existed between faculty and administrators. It was even better evidence of the ability of the administration and faculty to play a leadership role in the life of the university.

The developments which prompted the move to a senate organization and the adoption of a senate form of governance also prompted the change of name from the College of St. Thomas to the University of St. Thomas. This required board action and authorization by the state of Minnesota. The state requires only one graduate level program for an institution to be designated as a university and, as a matter of fact, it would have been possible to change the name in the early 1950s. However, St. Thomas waited until it had ten master's programs and three professional doctorates before doing this; it waited until it had truly grown into a university so that the name would be descriptive of the reality. The change in name also hastened the way the academic community looked at itself. While it wanted to retain the identity of the undergraduate college, at the same time it recognized that it had become a university. The new name prompted people to think in terms of St. Thomas' becoming an outstanding private university. More and more the university thought of itself as becoming a regional university of national quality. The Twin Cities lacked such a private university, and St. Thomas was intent on filling the vacuum. The board of trustees approved the change from college to university on May 3, 1990, and the state of Minnesota gave its authorization shortly thereafter.

An important factor in the successful reorganization was a widely shared understanding of the responsibilities of the various constitutive bodies of St. Thomas. No one of them wanted to decide alone what was best for it. Within each group—administration, faculty, board, students, alumni—leadership came forth and cooperated with others to give the university a new structure and a new positioning. Obviously, the relationships had a history of cordial cooperation. The lesson is that in order to have a healthy institution, leadership must be present in all its parts; and it is the responsibility of the president to lead in developing among all elements in the university a spirit of understanding, mutual respect, cooperation, and a common understanding of the Catholic

mission. Such a spirit is especially important in the relationship between the faculty and the board of trustees.

11

A Developing Administration

One group that certainly must have a clear grasp of the mission and identity of the university is the administration. It is so intimately interwoven with the fabric of the university that failure to understand or to believe in the mission is a prescription for failure. Since the president is the head of the administration, this may seem to be a truism. It nevertheless needs emphasis because the administration is scattered across the institution and is of key importance in setting the tone and direction. For it is administrators at various levels with whom faculty and students mostly interact. They can further the mission or possibly set it aside in their day-to-day work.

In an effort to improve the performance of administrators and to secure a degree of uniformity, St. Thomas began a program of training in 1965 with the chief administrators attending programs in Management by Objectives (MBO). More specialized programs followed. Some key personnel attended summer courses at Harvard on administration in higher education. These programs stressed definition of job, responsibilities, setting of goals and objectives, and measurements of performance. This gave a common mental framework to the staff and an agreement on procedures.

Before this time there had been a dozen offices reporting to the president, and it was evident that no more than four or five persons should report to a superior; more than that meant the span of oversight was too large to be effective. With twelve persons directly responsible to the president, he could not oversee them and, in effect, most of them were not being supervised. Consequently, they had an undue amount of independence and there was only limited teamwork. Yet none wanted to change their line of reporting. They thought it meant their job was being downgraded. Some asserted that a consolidation would be a violation of an agreement made with them at the time they were hired. Over time the lines of authority were reduced to the more traditional structure, so that only the academic, business, student, and development offices directly reported to the president.

Nonetheless, the organizational structure was never absolutized. People were always more important in attaining goals than were job descriptions or commonly accepted structures. A job was sometimes defined in terms of the strengths of a staff member or a weakness shored up by giving a specific responsibility to someone with the skills to handle it better. For example, the vice president for administration was not really interested in computers and technology; consequently, the computerization of the administration was given to another vice president who was eminently qualified in such matters. The important consideration was who was best qualified to get the job done. Sometimes there were questions of personalities that did not work well together. These situations could be painful for all parties and sometimes difficult to work out. Yet in such cases as well as in cases where someone was not adequate for the job—perhaps had failed to grow as the job grew and changed—dealing with the situation was necessary, and often when it was confronted, a solution became apparent.

The style of governance became one of extensive delegation on the part of the president to chief administrators. And giving the chief administrators freedom to act released a great deal of talent and energy. They developed great loyalty to the university and great satisfaction in their jobs because they had a sense of accomplishing something significant. The success of the policy of extensive delegation depended greatly on selecting the right persons for key positions, persons who were competent and willing to take on responsibility. At the same time, they had to have the confidence of the president and the assurance that he was not second-guessing their actions and decisions. They might make a decision that was not the kind of decision the president would have made, but it was generally better to have an action take place than to postpone a decision until the president could act. That would have slowed down the momentum of the administrator and taken the time of the president which could be better spent on matters he truly needed to handle.

A helpful practice was never to disagree with a staff person in public unless the mistake was so evident that others would interpret the silence as agreement or incompetence on the part of the president. Such situations almost never occurred. When a correction had to be made, it was made in private or, at most, at the president's staff meeting. On one occasion, for instance, an enthusiastic vice president took a matter for approval directly to the executive committee of the board of trustees without first consulting the president. Rather than undercut the credibility of the vice president before members of the board, the president let the matter be handled by the trustees, who assumed that the president supported the proposal. After the meeting and in private, the president discussed with the vice president his action and refused to implement the matter until there had been time to study it.

At the same time the administration's lines of command were being changed, the board of trustees was organized into standing committees which paralleled the major areas of the university, and the vice president responsible for the administration of an area served as staff person to the board committee. For example, the academic vice president was staff person to the academic affairs committee of the board and the vice president for business affairs was staff person for the investment committee. This worked well. It meant that each committee had the service of the person best informed about the area. It also meant that the vice president had input to and guidance from the committee. The president had to be close to both the committees and their staff persons in order to insure coordination of all the areas. His job was to bring together the work of all the committees. There could have been problems with committees short-circuiting the president and going directly to the board, but that rarely happened and was easily corrected. It is possible that a president lacking in self-confidence or feeling unsupported by the board could be uneasy with such a system.

A concern was that a vice president might reach a decision and then ask the committee to approve it. That would be a poor involvement of the trustees. They brought to deliberations an outsider's point of view which was helpful and important; however, the committee had to be given the opportunity and challenge to wrestle with problems, to think them through, bringing their own experience and competencies to bear, and only afterwards to reach a decision. When they had that degree of involvement, they took responsibility and initiative. The job of the staff person was to supply information, to present the issues and all the pertinent considerations, sometimes to indicate a preferred position, but then to let the trustees weigh the matter and come to a recommendation that could be taken to the full board. No committee made board policies or decisions. These were reserved for the entire board, except that the executive committee, which met monthly, could make decisions that could not be delayed until the next meeting of the full board. At forty-three members, the size of the board makes it difficult to hold meaningful discussions at meetings and consequently much of the work is necessarily done by the committees. This means that the staff work has to be of the highest quality to insure the excellence of the committee's recommendations.

Over the years the president's staff evolved. The positions of business manager and treasurer were combined into one, that of the vice president for business affairs. A vice presidency for student affairs was created to supervise the dean of students and the several offices which had grown out of the dean's office, such as student housing. A provost was appointed to supervise many of the day-to-day operations as the president became more and more caught up in major fund-raising, planning, and community relations. In many universities the position of provost has a strong orientation toward academic affairs; however, it can be defined in various ways. At St. Thomas, although the first provost had been academic vice president, the position was given wide responsibilities and was somewhat comparable to that of executive vice president.[1]

The creation of a competent and strong staff is a major responsibility of a president. One test of a staff's competency is how well it performs in the president's absence, especially during a long absence. If it carries on as usual, it is evident that the members of the staff know their jobs, have confidence they can do them, and have the delegated authority to make responsible decisions. It also means there is a qualified leader to step into the president's place to coordinate and direct the staff. If the president is little missed, it does not mean that he/she is not doing the job; on the contrary, it is a clear indication that he/she has done an excellent job in creating a staff that can run the administration even for longer periods of time. On two occasions the president of St. Thomas was absent for about three months, once because of illness, another time because he was on a sabbatical leave. On each occasion the university ran smoothly and maintained its momentum. Pity a poor president who cannot leave the university without worrying about what is happening on the home campus!

---

[1] In 1998 the position of provost was abolished and a new one, that of executive vice president, created.

Something of the same mind-set encountered among the various directors of administrative sections at an earlier time also existed among some chairpersons of St. Thomas academic departments who would remain the head until retirement. When a system of five-year terms was put in place, some objected: they saw it as a demotion. Limited terms, however, meant that different ideas could emerge, new endeavors could be undertaken. Since the members of the department were consulted on the appointment of the chairperson, a wide degree of participation and, in some instances, a sort of collective leadership became possible. Some departments formed committees to make recommendations on the granting of tenure; the basis of judgment was enlarged and the chairperson no longer had to shoulder alone the responsibility for tenure recommendations. As the faculty grew in number, some of these changes were helpful and perhaps even necessary.

The faculty came to share more fully in governance. For example, in appointed committees, as distinct from the committees of the faculty organization, which were elected, the faculty often elected a majority of the members of the committee and the president appointed the other members, whereas earlier he had appointed all the members. Over the years the structure of the university changed as circumstances changed, but it held fast to its values and mission. The effect was a better response to academic needs and to the needs of the community.

12

Institutional Culture, Entrepreneurship, and Communication

The changes described in the last chapter need to be seen in the context of the culture of St. Thomas. In recent years considerable attention has been paid to the culture of various organizations. For example, John P. Cotter and James L. Heskett have written on corporate culture, which they see as tremendously important to the success of an organization, even to understanding an organization.[1] It is at least equally important for universities. Catholicism is an integral part of the fundamental cultural values of St. Thomas and is treated throughout this study. At the operational level there are two important elements in its culture that deserve to be treated more fully. They are entrepreneurship and communication.

Higher education is generally thought not to be entrepreneurial. Rather, academicians tend to be cautious and to avoid taking unnecessary risks. An entrepreneurial culture developed at St. Thomas and became a distinctive characteristic. It led to many developments and deserves to be looked at carefully.

---

[1] John P. Cotter and James L. Heskett, *Corporate Culture and Performance* (New York: Free Press, 1992). See also Terrence E. Deal and Allan A. Kennedy, *Corporate Cultures* (Reading, Mass.: Addison-Westley, 1982).

For a long time there had been a willingness at St. Thomas to reach out to new ventures. One could possibly trace this back to the founder of the institution, Archbishop Ireland, who in his statements and actions was an innovator. In the 1920s St. Thomas established schools in law, engineering, and commerce (the first two of these failed during the Great Depression). Then, in a tentative way the university started a fifth-year program for teachers in the early 1950s. It was not a degree program, but provided courses required for teacher certification. It became a Master of Arts in Teaching (MAT) program and eventually led to a school of education offering eight master's, two doctorate, and an undergraduate program in elementary education. In 1964 St. Thomas established a major in journalism. This was followed by a degree in computer science. Both were unique among the private liberal arts colleges in the region.

So there was a precedent, even a tradition, of prudent risk-taking in innovating new programs. Perhaps this was one of the reasons a Carnegie study in 1965 referred to the College of St. Thomas as a "bellwether" among Catholic colleges. In 1962 the Ford Foundation had chosen St. Thomas as the first Catholic men's college to receive one of its matching challenge grants because it was a college on the move.

A considerable shift toward an entrepreneurial culture developed in the late 1970s when the White House held a nationwide conference on small businesses. Persons connected with the university participated, and the awareness of the importance of small business for the creation of jobs and of the economy grew on the part of St. Thomas leadership.

A major development came about when the Honeywell Corporation made a major matching grant for a chair in small business. In seeking the funds to match the grant, the university's personnel and its friends saw more clearly that small business is the wellspring of a free economy. The character growth that small business demands of those who would succeed in it is an important by-product. Soon other allied programs and chairs were created: a program in franchise business was established, and a program and chair in family business became very successful: family businesses often have problems of succession, and good long-range plans in place early on can help to avoid such problems while still providing for the continuity and development of the business. A program in entrepreneurship became nationally known, its graduates establishing outstanding records in starting and growing successful businesses. All these programs—in small business, entrepreneurship, franchising, and family business—have many things in common and strengthen one another. Together they give St. Thomas a commanding position in the development of entrepreneurial business. The university has gained national recognition for its work in encouraging and enabling small entrepreneurial business: in 1999 it was named the National Model Undergraduate Entrepreneurship Program by the United States Association for Small Business and Entrepreneurship.

Graduate courses in business are frequently taught by people who are themselves engaged in business, often at the senior level. This was not part of the original plan, but the adjunct faculty proved to be such good teachers and so popular with the students that their number grew. Since the program is designed for people who have already started their careers and are eager to advance in their chosen field, it has a very practical orientation directed toward application: people who are successful and knowledgeable in business are a natural "fit" and can make excellent teachers and models for their students. In addition, the university made an effort to hire as full-time faculty persons who had significant experience in business as well as academic training. There is no doubt that a faculty with considerable business involvement brought an understanding of entrepreneurship to their teaching and the programs they designed.

From this point it was a small step to inquiring whether entrepreneurship could enhance university leadership. The president decided to hire for leadership roles people who possessed or had the potential for entrepreneurship. This was a new criterion in hiring. And as people came to understand entrepreneurship and as the university looked for and encouraged innovative leadership, a number of new endeavors sprouted up: the education department launched satellite programs off campus, one as far away as California; an evening school for working people was started; a conference center was established sixty miles from campus; a whole new campus came into being in downtown Minneapolis. The university itself came to be looked upon as entrepreneurial and because of this attracted people of the same spirit. Thus, an entrepreneurial dimension was added to the culture of the university. Ideas for new programs or the improvement of existing ones emerged. There was excitement and confidence that the university was "on the move." The challenge was to encourage and feed the entrepreneurial spirit.

A strong entrepreneurial culture and successful leadership require good communication. This, in turn, requires openness and broad participation in decision making. However, not everyone who works at a university needs to be consulted on every decision. It is important to define who makes a decision, and that relates to who has the competency and the responsibility and who is affected by the decision. Not having a definition of responsibilities may result in the feeling that everyone is entitled to be consulted and counted when every decision is made, but there is often not the time to consult everyone who would like to be consulted. Besides, there is little use in consulting people who know little or nothing about the matter and who, in any case, are not responsible for the results. Yet it remains that if people expect to have a voice in a decision and are not given that voice, they are disappointed and frustrated. Hence, the importance of avoiding unreal expectations, and that requires a clear understanding of who will make decisions and in what areas.

In academic matters, faculty have extensive authority because of their collective competency. This is true across the country. Yet faculty sometimes think that decisions are made by "them," that is, the administration, and even made before they have been consulted. They can be suspicious and resistant, and the administration is guilty until proven innocent! There may be many reasons for this attitude: academicians are trained to be critical thinkers, and administrators often encounter difficulties in communicating with faculty. There is also among some faculty a simplistic notion of leadership. Faculty members who become administrators are often surprised by the complexity and the actual amount of consultation required in making decisions and getting them implemented.

Good communication requires much more than statements, even though the printed and spoken word are very important. The environment needs to be open and collaborative so that there is trust. In the absence of this, the communication is received but not taken at face value. Communication requires two parties, and if the recipient does not trust the writer or speaker, there is a serious block to its effectiveness. The person-to-person dimension is fundamental. That is why the president of a university—a symbol of the institution—should be seen and heard. He/she may be merely repeating information known by the hearers, but if the statement concerns core values commonly accepted by the listeners, then they are reassured.

Ultimately, the best means of communicating is involvement. People who invest their time and energy in a matter come to understand it better and to be committed to it. Faculty must be involved in the process of decision making. Committees are necessary to achieve good policies, to allow for a wide range of views, and to secure implementation of decisions. People are usually more willing to abide by decisions they or their representatives have helped make than decisions imposed "from above." While faculty frequently want to be involved, some resent the time taken from their teaching and research. At the same time, administrators should not be allowed to duck their responsibilities on the excuse that "the committee decided." Clearly, it is necessary to determine in advance what is advisory and what is decision making.

For St. Thomas and many universities, the acid test of communication was the student unrest over the Vietnam War, an era of great tension, conflict, and change for American higher education. Universities have not been the same since. A social revolution took place in American society and especially in higher education. The confluence of the civil rights movement and the anti-Vietnam War movement, the sexual revolution, the feminist rights movement, and for Catholic institutions, the Second Vatican Council—elements in each reinforcing one another—turned universities into battlegrounds, socially, intellectually, emotionally, and sometimes even physically. If these movements had occurred successively, their impact would have been vastly different; together they overloaded the system and endangered its leadership. The control and direction of higher education was in jeopardy. Only those who lived at the epicenter of this upheaval can really understand the tension and emotions and comprehend what was at stake.

Two incidents among many stand out at St. Thomas. One was an attempt by the militant Black Panthers to take over the campus. Representatives came on campus and arranged for a meeting at a later date with African-American students. The local police were notified, identified some of the leaders, and became greatly concerned. Preparations were made for police intervention at the time of the meeting, but only if it was absolutely necessary. The university's concern was to avoid a confrontation, and the visible presence of police on campus might have been a spark to set off a conflagration. Consequently, the administration asked the police not to come on campus or into the immediate surroundings, but to be ready to respond if it became necessary to call them.

The modus operandi of the Panthers called for a core of African-American students on campus to support them before they would try to take it over. The university relied on the good judgment of its students to refuse overtures from the Panthers. There obviously was a risk in a meeting between experienced militant activists and students who for the most part were not activists. It was a risk worth taking. At the same time, the administration was prepared to act, even to make arrests for trespassing if necessary, but that would be a last resort. Fortunately, good sense prevailed, and the students refused to cooperate with the Black Panthers, who then left the campus.

Another heightened moment was the incursion of the United States armed forces into Cambodia. In addition, President Nixon had indicated that students would not be able to avoid the draft after graduating from college. They could not continue to avoid serving in Vietnam because the reasons for deferment were to be greatly limited, such as attending graduate school or teaching in elementary or high schools. Tension intensified on campus. The very people who were most opposed to the war were now to have no escape. Their only alternative was to stop the war.

The shooting of protesters at Kent State University inflamed passions. Protests sprang up all over the nation. It was the most explosive moment at St. Thomas because it involved a large number of students in an all-male college (later it would become evident that there was coordination from outside). Protests, rallies, talk-ins were held across campus. The faculty was troubled and uncertain how to respond. The president held a convocation for all students where all points of view could be expressed. In the end the good sense of the community prevailed: there was no violence, and while hostility toward the war continued, calm eventually returned to campus.

A great deal of energy was spent during the Vietnam years just trying to keep the university from being torn apart, or at least from grinding to a halt. It was energy that in other times would have been spent in more constructive ways, yet it was energy well spent. For in some colleges the curriculum was changed to be less rigorous and less demanding of students; many of these institutions have not yet fully recovered. But St. Thomas, despite considerable pressure, held firm to its structured curriculum; its instructional program did not change, and work in the classroom went on. This was a significant accomplishment.

The experiences of the Vietnam era illustrate the absolute necessity of good communication. This begins with the president and other chief administrators being available to students, talking directly to them. The president is a symbol of the university and of its authority and thus must have the patience and forbearance to tolerate personal abuse from those who dislike "the system," to deal with unfounded and unfair criticism. He/she must be open and fair while stating the basic and traditional values of the university and yet be willing to consider and, when appropriate, to modify existing practices. In times of criticism faculty, too, need to hear the president articulate the values of the university.

The statements may contain no new information. What is important is that the faculty are reassured that the institution is solid and remains on course.

In the interest of improving personal communication, the president and chief administrators at St. Thomas set time aside each week to meet with students on a first-come, first-served basis. This open-door policy proved very effective. Students could also meet with any administrator at other times by appointment. Another channel of communication was the establishment of monthly meetings of the president and his chief administrators with the elected officers of the student government. The students set the agenda; administrators came to the meeting prepared to deal with the topics the students had chosen and any other topics that might arise. In addition, each semester the president held a student convocation. Administrators and students submitted a list of topics to the president. At the same time, the president had the opportunity to make a statement on whatever topics he chose. And there was always an opportunity for questions from the floor; students who otherwise might not be able to question the president had the opportunity to do so. The interest in these convocations was in direct proportion to the students' current interests: a "crisis" brought out a large number of students; in times of relative calm on campus, the convocation was less well attended.

These efforts at communicating not only informed, explained, and, hopefully, persuaded, but they also were safety valves which allowed any serious problem to emerge; they kept the administrators informed of students' concerns so that timely responses could be made when called for.

There were other avenues of communication that did not flow out of the Vietnam crisis and were not necessarily directed to students, but students usually had some involvement or representation. The president wrote a column for each issue of the school paper. A survey of these columns shows that they regularly dealt with very practical subjects of interest, especially to students. The provost held forums to discuss current topics. A review of the topics discussed is a good index of what was taking place in higher education around the country.

While the curriculum was not substantially revamped, as in so many colleges, there was an effort to afford students more opportunities to select professors, including professors at cooperating neighboring colleges. New academic majors were added, and in some instances new courses were added or existing courses revised to meet student interest as well as to incorporate changes in the academic discipline. The enlargement of choices certainly was an improvement and helpful in dealing with student criticism or unrest.

An administrative council was established, made up of administrators and representatives from the student body and the faculty. It was an effort to provide a means of participation in governance to the administrators and staff comparable somewhat to that enjoyed by the faculty through the faculty organization and to students through student government. It dealt with policies and gave a voice to the participants and kept them informed as well. As time went on, it concerned itself more and more with information on administrative matters and faculty and student interest waned.

Communication with faculty as well as faculty participation took place through regular administrative channels and through the long established faculty organization for governance. Its standing committees had various arrangements with the chief administrator in the area with which they dealt; for example, the Educational Policy Committee was chaired by the academic vice president. This system worked well.

However, from time to time there were faculty who were uneasy about the close arrangement with the administration or who felt adequate attention was not being given to their more personal concerns, such as salary and fringe benefits or various other issues. One can discern a pattern over the years. A few people would try to establish a chapter of the American Association of University Professors (AAUP). Organizational meetings, usually centering on some issue, would be held. If enough people were interested, a chapter would be formed, but generally it would peter out after a few meetings. This would be followed by an effort to establish a new standing committee within the faculty governance organization. If that effort was successful, the new committee would go on for some years and then lose its political base of support. For instance, the new committees sometimes dealt with perennial problem areas such as finances or enrollment; eventually faculty members would get tired of such problems and lose interest. Then after some time, the cycle would begin again.

There was a pattern in the membership. The people who proposed the committee were usually elected to serve on the committee since they were the most ardent and assertive champions of their cause. When their terms expired, the next group would be less forceful and more typical of the faculty. This is not to suggest that the early efforts were ever hostile in origin. They were generally constructive. In recent years, as the financial strength of the university improved, it was in a better position to deal with fringe benefits and similar interests of the faculty.

Many other means of communication were also developed. A publication called *The Muckraker* appears from time to time, which enables faculty and staff members to state their criticism of the university or of one another. Its value is more in enabling people to "sound off" than in any enlightenment it may shed on a topic. Now, with electronic communication, there is a constant forum available to everyone on e-mail. There are numerous other publications, some on a regular basis, some from time to time, which tell about various programs. An excellent alumni/ae magazine is published four times a year. There are two newspapers, one published by students, the other by the administration. There are televised programs produced by students and aired on a local cable channel. And the list goes on.

Communications and openness are prerequisites for an entrepreneurial culture.[2] A university with such a culture finds ways of expanding service to its constituents and to its community.

---

[2] Ibid.

III. Critical Decisions

13

A Study in Decision Making

Some changes are of far-reaching effect because they set in motion other changes or move a university in an important new direction or signal an attitude of openness to change. Their full impact may not be seen for several years. Such was the decision at St. Thomas to become coeducational at the undergraduate level, one of the most important changes in its history (see also the discussion of coeducation in chapter 7). It is a good example of how decisions were made. It was reached only after lengthy deliberation. A committee was formed in 1970 to study the possibility of becoming coeducational. Eventually there were three faculty and staff committees on this matter over a period of approximately five years. Visits were made to colleges that had recently become coeducational or were single sex and close neighbors to institutions that recently had become coeducational. Surveys were taken to get the reaction of prospective students, of current students, and of alumni.

A great deterrent was fear that if St. Thomas became coeducational, it would have a harmful impact on its sister institution, the College of St. Catherine. On November 25, 1975, St. Catherine's faculty passed a resolution asking St. Thomas not to become coeducational because it would be harmful to St. Catherine's. There was a long history of cooperation between the two institutions. In earlier years much of it had consisted of student social events; more recently there were major efforts to cooperate in both faculty and student exchanges, and class schedules and offerings were coordinated or combined. In 1976, the *Minneapolis Star* (Oct. 20) reported that 1,609 St. Catherine students took courses at

St. Thomas and 1,298 St. Thomas students took courses at St. Catherine's. It seemed that much of what was being achieved through cooperation would be jeopardized by a decision to become coeducational. Many alumni of St. Thomas were married to alumnae of St. Catherine's, and there was considerable overlap among the financial supporters of both institutions. The reaction of these people might be negative. Moreover, the conventional wisdom was that alumni generally were opposed to men's colleges becoming coeducational. It was assumed they wanted the college to remain as they remembered it from their student days. However, a survey of the alumni showed that they favored accepting women by a two to one margin. On reflection, this did not seem surprising because the alumni wanted their daughters as well as their sons to receive the kind of education they had received. What had happened was a shift in the kind of education that they wanted for their daughters and that their daughters wanted. St. Thomas' curriculum reflected the all-male makeup of its student body: it had strength in fields which were opening up more and more to women, for example, business, computer science, journalism, medicine. At the same time, many women wanted to go to a coeducational institution; they did not want to be in a women's college during their undergraduate years. But there was no coeducational Catholic college in the Twin Cities; they had to go out of the area, and for a variety of reasons, that was often not acceptable or possible.

Surprisingly, the student body, which earlier had favored coeducation, switched its position and opposed it as the time for a decision drew near. It is difficult to know what prompted that shift, perhaps the influence of a few leaders. At some colleges which had become coeducational there was resentment toward women as they moved into facilities and endeavors that had been male preserves. In any case, the opposition was not strong.

The board of trustees created a committee to study the matter and make a recommendation. It included the former president of a women's college, whose term began immediately after the college's neighboring all-male institution became coeducational. He stated that his institution enjoyed its most prosperous days after this event: among other things it launched a series of new programs that met the needs of contemporary women. The committee also included a provost of a university formed by the merger of a women's college and a men's college. The board made an effort to have every point of view represented. After careful inquiry and consideration, the committee recommended that St. Thomas become coeducational. The board of trustees then directed its executive committee to consult with representatives of the College of St. Catherine and to get their response to such a decision. It reported back to the board in September 1977, and the final decision was made to become coeducational.

In implementing this change, great effort was made to avoid the problems that plagued other men's colleges that had become coeducational. At some, women received the least attractive living accommodations, often on the periphery of the campus, because the men were unwilling to give up the residences they occupied. That problem was avoided at St. Thomas by building a new residence hall for women. In some institutions faculty who had grown accustomed to teaching only men had difficulty adjusting to the new classroom environment. At St. Thomas women had attended classes under the exchange arrangement with other colleges for several years; consequently, the faculty had become accustomed to teaching women and men together.

In order not to cause dislocations at St. Catherine's, the college adopted two policies: not to accept immediately transfer students from St. Catherine's and not to start programs that were traditionally open to women and available at St. Catherine's. It turned out that the impact of the decision had no or little negative effect on St. Catherine's. Fears of hurting the college were ungrounded. Another evidence of male chauvinism!

As pointed out earlier in making the decision to become coeducational, there had been wide consultation and participation. The faculty and administration had initiated the process jointly and together had explored the possibilities. Considerable time was taken to study the matter. Not just faculty and staff, but students, alumni, and friends, were involved, as well as the governing board. Most important, the decision was not prompted by necessity. Enrollment was growing, not declining. The number of freshmen in the fall of 1975 was at a near all-time high, 659 freshmen, although in the immediately preceding years there had been a decline in freshmen; and the total enrollment was almost 4,000 students, with 2,390 undergraduates. In addition, the university's finances were solid and improving.

Key factors, discussed previously, in favor of becoming coeducational were the desire to improve the educational experience for men and to provide a Catholic coeducation for women who could not obtain it locally. But the driving force behind these was the conviction that a Catholic education has great advantages and should be made available to as many persons as possible. There were other reasons as well. The committee of visitors appointed by the board of trustees recommended that St. Thomas "seek to provide through new arrangements creative opportunities to deepen understanding between the sexes and provide a more realistic setting for our students."[1] The report further stated, "It is seriously questioned whether the sexes should be isolated at the college level during the crowning phase of their intellectual, emotional, and cultural development when there is the risk that merely superficial contact on a social level may perpetuate stereotyped sex roles."[2]

Behind the interest in providing a Catholic liberal arts education to more people and in doing it in a more natural and balanced environment, there were undoubtedly other motives. The dean of students urged coeducation as a means to improve retention. There were national and state forecasts of a declining number of high school graduates beginning in 1979, and this raised questions about the size of future enrollment. The Minnesota Higher Education Coordinating Commission forecast a drop in high school graduates from 74,180 students in 1979 to 45,000 students in 1991. The chairperson of the Minnesota state committee to establish a new statewide system of community colleges pointed out that the thirty-seven community colleges would have an adverse impact on the enrollments of the private colleges in the state. That, in turn, engendered anxiety about St. Thomas' future financial stability. It was also a time when there was a push for the adoption of an equal rights amendment which, with certain judicial interpretations, might restrict financial assistance to universities that were not open to all students, regardless of gender.

A strong case could be made for women's colleges on the grounds that some women, but not all, prefer and actually perform better in a single-sex environment, where their talents for leadership can flourish in a climate not dominated by men. No similar rationale can be made for a men's institution—there really was no case to be made for an all-men's college. Even men who were opposed to St. Thomas' becoming coeducational said, according to a survey, they would still enter the college if it became coeducational, while a significant number of women indicated they would enroll if it became coeducational.

It was easy to measure the impact of women on campus in terms of growth. More difficult was the problem of separating the influence of

[1] John Daly, S.J., and others, "Coeducational Feasibility Study," 15 January 1976, University of St. Thomas Archives, p. 13.

[2] Ibid., 10.

coeducation from other developments taking place at the same time. The retention rate, that is, the percentage of students who persevered until graduation, increased considerably. Certainly there was a dramatic increase in the number of students transferring to St. Thomas from other colleges. Were these developments due to the changed social environment brought on by the presence of women?

There were some indications that the first women to enroll were venturesome, desirous of being the "first" and of breaking down barriers. They established outstanding records in women's athletics and were also successful in getting elected to offices in student activities and organizations including class presidencies and the presidency of the student body. Very soon a woman was chosen by the student body to receive the "Tommy" award, given to the outstanding student of the year.

What about the question raised by the committee of visitors concerning "whether sexes should be isolated at the college level during the crowning phase of their intellectual, emotional, and cultural development when there is a risk that merely superficial contact on a social level may perpetuate stereotyped sex roles"? No scientific study at St. Thomas has been done on this question, but an anecdote may give some insight.

One day the president of the college was stopped on campus by a senior faculty member who said, as nearly as the president remembers: "I was opposed to St. Thomas becoming coeducational. Two of my sons attended St. Thomas when it was an all-male place; one attended after it became coeducational. As I look now at the development of my three sons, I am persuaded that my third son who received his education after we became coeducational had the best experience. I have changed my mind and I now favor coeducation."

It is clear that the decision for St. Thomas to become coeducational was fundamentally important and was made only after a careful open process in which all constituencies of the university participated. Its consequences were far-reaching: it greatly enlarged the pool of prospective students; the undergraduate student body almost doubled in size; more students received a Catholic education. It was the first of several endeavors that expanded the pool of prospective students and greatly changed the university. Its impact, however, was more than just the enrollment of more students. In reversing an important policy that established an identifying characteristic of St. Thomas for almost one hundred years, it had a significant influence in creating a climate of movement, of openness to new ideas and new possibilities. In this process the university held fast to its historical values—Catholic and liberal arts education—while at the same time displaying a remarkable degree of adaptability.[3] This gave a sense of confidence that the institution would continue to adapt to changing circumstances and to fulfill its mission to the church and community at large.

---

[3] See Robert Birnbaum, *How Academic Leadership Works* (San Francisco: Jossey-Bass, 1992) 97–104.

14

Why Business Administration?

The open and participatory decision-making process which resulted in St. Thomas' becoming coeducational was also followed in
other decisions of fundamental importance. One was to establish a
graduate program in management, which led to significant developments at the post-baccalaureate level. Another was to build a campus in
downtown Minneapolis; heretofore, St. Thomas was located only in St.
Paul. Both of these decisions will be looked at more closely because they
illustrate the university's commitment to certain values, especially religious values, and its willingness to take prudent risks in the interest of
serving the broader community.

St. Thomas' department of business administration has a long history, almost as long as the institution itself. When the university began
as St. Thomas Aquinas Seminary in 1885, it had the dual purpose of
training men for the priesthood or of preparing them for such professions as law and medicine. After the seminary moved to a separate
campus in 1894, more attention was given to teaching "commerce,"
probably as a means of replacing the seminarians who had left. This was
at a time when liberal arts colleges rarely taught business, regarded as a
poor cousin to the liberal arts. Yet the clientele of the university was
composed of the sons and grandsons of poor immigrants. The city of
St. Paul itself had its greatest growth at the end of the nineteenth and
beginning of the twentieth century when immigrants and their children
came into the area in large numbers. As their history would show, they
had a strong desire to move up the economic and social ladder, and
education, especially in business, was a key to upward mobility.

Business education continued to grow at St. Thomas, and became one of the most popular academic fields for the student body. By the late 1950s it was the largest major in the university. This growth reflected a national trend and a great opportunity for an institution concerned about the quality of life in its community.

When master's programs in business administration were springing up around the country, the department of business recommended the establishment of a graduate program in business management. This ran contrary to a firmly established policy of concentration on undergraduate education in the conviction that limited resources should be used to improve undergraduate education. An exception had been made to that policy in the early 1950s in the field of teacher training in response to the needs of nuns teaching in Catholic schools.

A limited survey of interest in a graduate degree in business administration was done among the business community, with inconclusive results. One of the largest employers said it had no interest in such a program; nevertheless, the business department continued to press for its establishment. Then the president, the academic vice president, and the chair of the department of business set out to visit as many MBA programs as was necessary to learn whether St. Thomas was ready to offer a master's degree in business administration. Along the way they learned a great deal about business schools.

One of the schools visited was in many ways similar to St. Thomas. It was basically a Catholic liberal arts university with a few graduate programs. Its MBA program, led by a very competent and entrepreneurial dean, was large and successful. The university was located in a metropolitan area similar to the Twin Cities—the center of a large trade area with a great number of different businesses whose corporate headquarters were located there. Moreover, there was a large tax-supported university with an MBA program in the same city. Yet seemingly contrary to the common opinion that small private institutions should not try to compete against large, well-established, tax-supported ones, the program was thriving and larger than that of the state university.

A basic question that had to be answered remained: Why should St. Thomas depart from its policy of concentrating, with one exception, on undergraduate education? Some faculty feared that resources would be drained away from liberal arts; they also saw business education, especially at the post-baccalaureate level, as almost antithetical to liberal education—such education at its worst was positivistic and materialistic and therefore did not belong in their kind of institution. The result was tension within the college.

Yet there were very good reasons to start an MBA program, consistent with the mission of the university. Service to the community, for instance, had long been an integral part of the mission, which in recent years had become even more prominent, and there appeared to be a need for a program of a special type, one that would be complementary to, and not competitive with, that of the University of Minnesota, the only MBA program in the metropolitan area. This was a daytime program which had an enrollment of perhaps two hundred to three hundred full-time students, was oriented to theory, and gave preference to those who intended to earn a doctorate in business. Yet the Twin Cities had a wide range of businesses such as computer manufacturing and software development, grain and food processors and distributors, retail stores, large manufacturers like 3M and Honeywell, and the list goes on. These and other international, national, and regional companies, many with corporate headquarters located in the metropolitan area, needed talented employees trained in business and administration. In addition, Minnesotans put a high value on education, and there was reason, therefore, to believe that a large number would welcome the opportunity to continue their education while working, in order to improve their skills and knowledge in ways that would advance their business careers and enrich their lives. It clearly appeared there was a need to be met in the community—an opportunity for St. Thomas to serve a new and important constituency.

But what about the conflict with the liberal arts? What was needed was an MBA program that incorporated many of the elements of a liberal arts education. The goal would be to produce people who were broadly educated and therefore generalists in the sense that good managers and leaders must be generalists and not just narrow specialists. Manager-leaders are decision makers, and the broader their education, the more they are able to see a problem or opportunity in a wide context, the greater the likelihood they will make good decisions. The program would be designed to include religious values and humanistic dimensions, the better to equip people to be leaders with compassion and concern for others, people who would understand the social role of business and its stake in a democratic, free-enterprise system that can provide a rising standard of living for everyone. Such a program would see the goal of business to be profit, but also the service of all who are engaged in the business—all the "stakeholders," that is, stockholders, employees, customers, and the community.

An integral part of the MBA would be business ethics. It would not be sufficient to make a course in business ethics available, although that would be done. Rather, ethics would be integrated into other courses as well, for example, marketing, but especially into those dealing with policy-making. This program could produce a moral leader of high competency in business. Leaders of this caliber are needed because business has an enormous influence on the development of people; the environment in which the latter make their living shapes their lives, their attitudes, their actions. A common phenomenon is the separation of one's private life from one's public life: moral considerations are not brought into the marketplace. Whatever temporary gains there may be by this schizophrenic posture, the long-range results for the individual and the community are human impoverishment. Any education intended to improve the community should include ethical considerations, and a professedly religious institution is best able to provide such an education. Indeed, people expect it to do so. Thus, St. Thomas' religious commitments and its religious mission would be served by an MBA program characterized by an emphasis on humanistic and ethical concerns.

The business management area is of great importance if only because so many young people enter it. It takes young college graduates and influences them in many ways, in their ethics, in their view of what is success in life, of how people are to be treated, of what one's social responsibilities are. The slow and steady inculcation of its attitudes and practices has an enormous impact on the graduates and on society in general. The adage that one becomes what one does has a great deal of truth in it. Business policies and practices can reinforce or they can negate much of what is taught in home and school.

Besides the perceived conflict with the liberal arts, another objection to the university's offering the MBA was the possibility that the highly visible presence of a graduate business program in a Catholic university might be criticized as an endorsement of a lifestyle that lacks idealism and even glorifies materialism, that in the end leads to the worship of the god Mammon. Questionable practices have long plagued business and tarnished its image; some graduate schools of business have been censured for their failure to teach ethical business standards and concern for the common good.

The public has a right to expect standards of decency on the part of business leaders. Instead of standing aside and ignoring the moral lapses of some business leaders, universities should prepare young people for moral leadership within business. In the long run a business will prosper to the degree it serves society, and that means it needs people of integrity and leadership ability. Universities that produce such people render a great service to their individual graduates and to the community, which needs a healthy economy. The American economy is always on trial, always being tested to prove its worth. It proves its worth when it serves well.

Business produces the means which make possible a decent standard of living and cultural, social, and political advances. Without the wealth that business produces, much of the attractiveness and benefits of our society would be absent. Business is both a profession and a vocation: it is a calling that enables persons to be their brother's and sister's keeper in a special way because the primary purpose of business is service. Profit is necessary, of course, but it is not the primary reason for business. Competition in a free market produces good results but if left completely unregulated by concerns for the common good, there can be disastrous results. A business career can provide an excellent opportunity for stewardship, for the exercise of social responsibility, and for service to one's neighbor.

St. Thomas had resources that could be used to develop an MBA program. It had well-qualified people in both its undergraduate business and economics departments who were capable of teaching at the graduate level. What was needed was a dean who understood the kind of program needed and was capable of championing it both within and outside the university. A careful search found such a person. He had taught in the program after which St. Thomas' would be modeled. He had extensive training in philosophy and theology, as well as the liberal arts in general, and held a doctorate in business. He also had a proven track record as dean of a business school in a comparable university.

When all these elements were considered, the decision to start an MBA program was relatively easy to make. The department of business was large and influential within the faculty and successfully led it to support the program even though some remained reluctant. Interestingly, an opinion that emerged within the faculty was that this matter was not a faculty matter, but rather one for the board of trustees, which had to decide if it could provide the necessary resources. The proposal for the program had come from some faculty members; it had been discussed at length among the whole faculty which gave it broad support. It was anchored in the commitment to serve and allied with the liberal arts and religious values. And it seemed to be a natural extension of the strong undergraduate programs in business and economics.

There was a need. The fit with the university was good. The motive was to serve the community in an important way that could better the lives of people. It would be not just any kind of service, but one that accorded well with the university's Catholic character. The board of trustees gave unanimous approval.

From the beginning the program was a success. Using standards based on experience around the country, it was estimated the enrollment might reach between five and six hundred students. When it reached one thousand to eleven hundred, the dean estimated it was at its maximum and would probably decline. The program was expanded to include business communications in 1984 and international management in 1985. By the fall of 1992 the enrollment was just over three thousand, making it the second largest graduate school of business in the country after New York University.

Fears that resources would be taken away from the undergraduate college proved completely unfounded. New sources of money came forth, and the program paid its own way: it neither took money from other parts of the university nor added money to other areas. But it clearly helped the university to become better known. Fewer than five percent of its MBA students graduated from St. Thomas as undergraduates: a new constituency was developed. Surveys indicated that the presence of graduate programs was a major influence in choosing St. Thomas on the part of freshmen. There was also a significant increase in transfers from other colleges, many of whom were majors in business. This seems to indicate at least an indirect result of the success of the graduate business programs.

Similarly, the large increases in capital contributions appeared to be related in some degree to the new programs for the community, among which graduate business is the largest. Corporate business contributions in the 1960s were quite meager; the capital campaign at the end of the 1970s did better. However, the capital campaign at the end of the 1980s, by which time graduate business programs were excelling, did much better in business contributions than in any previous campaign.

The master's degree at St. Thomas requires the study of business ethics. Ethics is a component of the introductory course required of all students and also of the capstone course at the end of their study. In between there are ethical considerations that relate to many subjects, for example, finance and marketing. The David and Barbara Koch Endowed

Chair in Business Ethics supports a renowned ethicist who guides other faculty in their handling of ethical material. Moreover, working with business leaders, the university drew up a set of ethical principles and guidelines for international business.[1] This immediately caught on in many parts of the world as well as in the United States. Business people in Japan and in Europe found it very helpful. It has also been the subject of discussion at annual meetings of business leaders from all parts of the world which are held in Caux, Switzerland.[2]

The liberal arts have been brought into the classroom in various ways. Perhaps the most explicit and innovative is the establishment of a credit course comprised of the great books as taught at the Aspen Institute in Colorado and pioneered by Robert Hutchins and Mortimer Adler at the University of Chicago. It is clear that the religious and liberal arts mission of St. Thomas is not set aside in the graduate-level professional programs. Its graduate business school is known for its interest in business ethics and for the humanistic content of its courses, which give breadth of knowledge and at the same time bring the student face-to-face with great minds of the past, men and women who wrestled with the perennial questions of human existence.

Other institutions in the vicinity followed with programs geared to employed adults. The result is a much greater range of educational opportunities available in the community. The private institutions have demonstrated an ability to produce innovative ways to meet community needs and, in the process, have strengthened themselves.

The desire to reach out and serve the community and to do so in a way that integrates humanistic and religious commitments with professional education moved the university in new and important ways. The development was incremental, but the increments were large and prompted not by a grand vision of growth of the institution, but by a conviction that the church should be in the marketplace. Conviction, commitment, and willingness to serve rather than a grand plan were the guiding lights.

---

[1] *Minnesota Principles* (Minneapolis: Center for Ethical Business Cultures, 1992).

[2] *Caux Round Table Principles for Business Conduct,* Caux Institute for Corporate Responsibility, Minneapolis (Washington, D.C., 1995). These are a development of the *Minnesota Principles,* which were formulated by the Minnesota Center for Corporate Responsibility (now known as the Center for Ethical Business Cultures) at the University of St. Thomas. The *Minnesota Principles* have been published in 12 languages.

15

A New Campus Is Born

Over the years St. Thomas has established, as part of its outreach efforts, two campuses and several satellite locations in addition to its main campus in St. Paul. One campus is located in Owatonna, a thriving community in southern Minnesota. The other is in the center of downtown Minneapolis. The most interesting satellite is in the Mall of America—the largest shopping mall in the United States.

The business center of the region is clearly Minneapolis and its suburbs. So it was to be expected that more graduate students, especially in business, would come from west of the Mississippi River than from St. Paul and its suburbs. The situation in the area was unusual and probably unique. The Twin Cities metropolitan area was the only urban area of its size (2.5 million people) without a genuine private university (by the happenstance of history, some colleges had been named universities). The city of Minneapolis had just one small liberal arts college. None of the private institutions addressed forcefully the needs of the Minneapolis community, certainly not its business needs.

Experience with employed part-time graduate students shows that convenience and easy accessibility are major concerns for them. They are usually in the thirty-year age bracket, are working full-time, and many are married. They want an opportunity for education near where they work or live. Downtown Minneapolis seemed to be a logical place to hold classes. The pastor of a downtown church, who was a member of the board of trustees, proposed a partnership between his parish and St. Thomas which would involve a sharing of land, one parcel owned by the church and the other adjacent parcel to be purchased by the university.

The central location of this land made the prospect of building there attractive; also the pastor who suggested it thought the church and the university together would provide a heightened religious presence in the heart of downtown Minneapolis. It was an exciting, forward-looking idea, but when it was presented to the board of trustees, they voted it down—it seemed too big an undertaking. In retrospect that decision may have been wise: at that time the university's graduate programs were not well developed; financial resources also needed more cultivation.

While the specific project was turned down, the concept of a Minneapolis campus was alive. The seed had been planted. Certain members of the board would bring it up from time to time. As time went on, the makeup of the board gradually shifted to a majority coming from Minneapolis, not by any conscious design, but because community leadership more and more came from there. Finally, as business programs grew larger and began to crowd facilities in St. Paul, it seemed time to offer classes in Minneapolis. A board member offered free space in an old department store building in downtown Minneapolis for a limited time, and a foundation provided money for a survey of opinion on support in the downtown community. It revealed strong support. Money for the necessary modifications in the building to make it suitable for classrooms was sought from the Minneapolis business community. Here was an opportunity to test the prospects for financial support: with relatively little effort, approximately $500,000 was raised; all signals were go.

Courses began in the spring of 1987, with an expected enrollment of between 100 and 150 students. In the first semester there were 306 students and the numbers continued to grow until by the fourth year there were 1,000 students. Clearly a need was being met.

Later, the building in which the classes were located was scheduled to be torn down. Although it would have been possible to continue in downtown Minneapolis by renting space, St. Thomas wanted to do more than merely make classes available—it wanted to become a permanent member of the Minneapolis community. The safest thing would have been either to rent space or to construct a building that could easily be converted to business offices if the academic program should wane. That course of action was decided against because the university wanted to make a clear statement that it intended to be a long-term player in the city. And this suggested not just a classroom building but a campus—at a minimum a city block of property—a difficult acquisition in a downtown area. The style of architecture was to be traditionally collegiate, in the neo-Gothic style, and built with the same kind of stone used on the parent campus in St. Paul. The idea was to construct a complete campus in downtown Minneapolis and thereby add a new institution to the city, with the many facilities and resources a university can provide. It would not be limited to business education, but would have a wide range of academic programs. It would be a dramatic statement to the community of an intention to contribute to its well-being.

Obviously, considerable risk was involved. No private university in the country had built a new campus in a downtown area in recent years. It was a time of financial restraints for higher education and not one for new and vast undertakings of a permanent nature. The initial cost was considerable, by far the most expensive project ever undertaken by the university.

An entire block of property plus some additions in the surrounding area—all in a prime location near the center of the city—were costly. The acquisition of this land required the cooperation of the city council and mayor. Compromises had to be made on all sides. The city wanted the university's graduate school of management to be located in Minneapolis; the university agreed to this. In return, the city agreed to dedicate some of its income from a tax increment development to help retire over the years the bonds sold to purchase the property. These were issued under the auspices of the Minnesota Higher Education Facilities Authority so that the interest paid on them was exempt under both state and federal tax laws. Consequently, the interest rate paid on the bonds was lower than it would have been if the interest had been taxable—a considerable benefit for St. Thomas.

To build public opinion and political support, conferences were held with representatives from the city's news media which led to their support in news stories and editorials. The Chamber of Commerce and other influential groups also backed the endeavor. The merits of the case were convincing and the university presented it in a straightforward manner, relying on the reasonableness of all parties. There is strong leadership in downtown Minneapolis that is determined to make the center of the city a vibrant business, cultural, and entertainment area. The leaders appreciated the help that St. Thomas would provide to raise the educational level of people living in Minneapolis and its suburbs. A better-educated population would mean a better and more prosperous community. Minneapolis, lacking a center-city private university, welcomed the opportunity to have a new institution at its core providing new opportunities for its citizens.

Once the way was cleared to buy the land, money had to be raised for the first building. Because it would have to contain many facilities in addition to classrooms and offices, such as a library, a bookstore, a dining area, an auditorium, and some parking space, it would be twice the size of the largest building on the St. Paul campus and several times more expensive. The most likely sources of money for the building were the businesses and foundations in Minneapolis. Again, the approach to potential donors was a forthright statement of the benefits to the city and its people. Care was taken not to overstate the case: no hype, no superlatives, no promises that would not be fulfilled. There was only an effort to convince people of the advantages they would enjoy. There was also St. Thomas' successful track record during its years in downtown Minneapolis; moreover, the university was known for its stability, strength, quality, and entrepreneurship. It was regarded as friendly toward business and government, concerned for city problems, such as the homeless and the poor in general. All in all, it was known as a place on the move, innovative, entrepreneurial, with a strong commitment to serve. It had an air of excitement and energy about it, and its record bred confidence and hope for the future. This ethos supported the fundamental reasonableness of its proposal, giving people confidence that what the university proposed to do, it could and would do.

There was considerable risk in trying to raise the amount of money needed for the new campus. St. Thomas had long been regarded as a small institution in St. Paul with only a limited relationship to Minneapolis, and the leadership in Minneapolis largely ignored St. Paul. The Mississippi River dividing the two cities was broad indeed! Besides, St. Thomas' record in raising money in Minneapolis was anything but encouraging. For one thing, only one or two Catholics had held leadership positions in the city's business community. However, by the time the university started to consider the new campus, many Catholics were leaders in business and government; they could help make the case for St. Thomas. Since the university was in the final stage of a major capital fund-raising effort, it could not go back to some of its traditional supporters but had to rely on new friends for large gifts. Undertaking to raise money for everything—land, building, and equipment—was a great challenge.

The community responded generously: the goal was reached, the land cleared, the building constructed; and classes began in September

1992. The enrollment of new students also increased, with a total of seventeen hundred. The Minneapolis campus was off to a grand start. Furthermore, during the course of the planning, an anonymous donor gave a magnificent gift of ten million dollars, the largest gift St. Thomas had ever received. While it was designated for programs in business education and not for construction costs, the university's development in Minneapolis undoubtedly encouraged the donor to make the gift.

As one looks back upon the process, it is clear that there was more risk involved than in any of the institution's previous endeavors except for its founding. The cost of land, building, and equipment was approximately twenty-eight million dollars; by the end of the debt repayment, the cost will have been more than fifty million. The board of trustees at first considered a Minneapolis campus as too risky an undertaking. The uncertainty was considerably reduced by becoming involved in the community. The market was tested by offering courses. People who were active in the community and known for their keen understanding of the sentiments of the people and for their knowledge of the city were consulted. Eventually there developed a conviction that the time was right and the circumstances propitious to move ahead in a step-by-step fashion. The decision, arrived at only after coming to know a great deal about every facet of the enterprise, based more on intelligence, experience, and judgment than on an accumulation of data analysis and projections, was intuitive (more right brain than left brain).

It was also opportune in that it was taken at a time when the membership of the city council was well disposed, as it might not have been even a few years earlier. There was a mood of openness and change abroad in the city as it sought to rejuvenate its downtown area. St. Thomas was enjoying a new level of acceptance in the city and beyond, but there was nothing in the university's long-range plan that called for a Minneapolis campus. There was only a fortuitous convergence of several factors that together provided an opportunity which previously had not been present. It was a moment which called for leaders and not just managers. The decision was broadly based, supported by faculty, staff, trustees, and the community. It was clearly related to the mission of the institution because it was grounded in a desire to serve, that is, to provide the kind of value-centered education the academic community believed in. It also gathered support from a large number of Catholics who saw it as a sort of "missionary" endeavor. As the institution entered new territory where it was largely unknown, its core religious elements were vital in this extension of its outreach.

It was an interesting process to watch as a nonprofit institution served as a leader and a catalyst in bringing together the people and resources needed to launch a new institution. It brought talent from outside the community, but much of the financial resources came from the community itself. The power of an idea stood forth as did the attractiveness of a strong commitment to serve, to help build better people for a better community, and a record of consistent achievement. The process, a long and careful one, was essentially the same as that by which St. Thomas decided to become coeducational, namely, an open and broad participation by all who had a stake in the matter. The risks were recognized and carefully weighed. The motivation was a desire to serve the community arising from a conviction of the worth of the kind of business education which is grounded on moral and religious values.

16

What Has Technology to Do with the Humanities?

In the 1980s Minnesota was quite conscious of its dearth of engineering schools and engineers. The University of Minnesota offered degrees in engineering and produced excellently trained engineers, but there were not enough of them to meet the needs of the state. Minnesota was an importer of engineering talent. This was particularly restrictive for smaller businesses, that is, those hiring one to three engineers and unable to compete with the large companies for talent. Yet the record of small business as a source of new jobs in the state is impressive. Minnesota wanted—needed—to encourage and support small businesses.

Minnesota must rely heavily on an educated work force. Its mines and forests are diminished. It still has good farmland in certain parts of the state, but it must rely increasingly on commerce and on manufacturing as essential elements of its economy. Its industries needed skilled people in the 1980s. At the same time, there were signs that its computer manufacturing industry, which had been a source of a great number of jobs, was beginning to falter. Was there a role for St. Thomas in dealing with these problems?

The governor agreed to host a dinner at the university for the CEOs of the largest manufacturers, and they were asked to identify their needs. One problem that emerged during the discussion was the unavoidable obsolescence of engineers' training: a few years after leaving school, they were in danger of becoming out-of-date and, as a result, their productivity and creativity declined to the detriment of their company and of their own careers. Providing the means for them to keep current in their fields would be a great service to them, their companies, and the community. Was this something a small institution without an engineering school could do?

A bit of advice offered by the guests at the dinner was that while there would be great growth in the computer software applications business, there would be considerably less need to engineer new computers. Moreover, there was a need in the area of manufacturing, especially in the application of advanced technology, particularly computers, to the manufacturing process. Nonetheless, the advice of all but one of the CEOs was very discouraging: the task and costs were too big for a private institution to undertake. There had been a similar experience in regard to the establishment of a master of business administration degree. Leaders in a couple of major businesses were not encouraging, even advised against starting an MBA. Once the MBA degree was established, however, one of these companies became a leading supporter. Proposed graduate programs in business and in engineering had initially met discouragement from leaders in their fields. Their initial reluctance to encourage the proposed program in business and engineering is a gauge of the degree of risk involved and of the complexity of the decisions involved in undertaking such programs. Yet both of these turned out to be exceedingly successful.

Following the meeting with the CEOs about needs, the university continued discussions at lower levels, that is, with the presidents and vice presidents of the companies represented at the governor's dinner. Gradually the consultation expanded and went on for approximately two years. At the end it was clear that while the education of new engineers was necessary, the most urgent need was for a program that enabled working engineers to keep up on new developments in their fields. It was a commonly held opinion that only a few universities in the country were capable of providing such education because these developments were taking place in the factories, at the workbenches, and in the laboratories, not in academia. Consequently, so it was said, it was not possible to hire teachers who were truly at the developing edge of a field; they simply were not available and the equipment was too costly. Besides, the only way to begin was with an undergraduate program and then grow into graduate studies.

Approximately two hundred persons were drawn into the consultative process. At its end, about fifty people volunteered to teach, on an adjunct basis, in a new master's degree program for engineers who were employed. They saw the need and were excited about the possibility of being part of a new program unlike any other, at least in Minnesota. Moreover, companies with highly specialized equipment offered to make it, as well as their employees, available for the instruction of graduate students. Contrary to the view of some that manufacturers would carefully guard their know-how lest competitors profit from it, many were eager to share and to help others learn the new things they were doing. They had the vision to recognize that sharing knowledge of state-of-the-art technology in manufacturing was good for the community and ultimately for everyone. Consequently, the specialized equipment needed for the program was available at manufacturing sites. Only the equipment found in any good programs at other universities was required at the home institution.

But before any decision could be made, some questions had to be answered: How does an engineering program relate to the liberal arts and religious mission of St. Thomas? Why should St. Thomas have a graduate program in engineering? Could liberal and humane education be integrated into the regular curriculum in engineering? In large measure the answer to these questions would depend on who directed the program and who taught in it since the subject matter probably lent itself directly to the humanities and religious values in only a limited way.

The program contemplated, at least in the beginning, was in manufacturing engineering. Such an enterprise called for pioneering in an area that was not widely taught as a formal discipline in schools of engineering. While that increased the risk of failure, it also enhanced the possibility of making a significant contribution in an area critical to the future of our country.

For a long time jobs in the manufacturing industry had been going to countries with capable people and low labor costs. This rush to offshore was causing serious unemployment and industrial dislocation. The answer was not to create trade barriers but to increase the productivity of American workers so that the products they produced would be competitive. It might also mean a shift to industries that needed more skilled, better-educated people. At the same time, manufacturers had exhibited an interest in integrating higher technologies into their work. A program in engineering that significantly incorporated the use of computers and other new technology in the manufacturing process could make a contribution to human well-being in providing employment and quality products at competitive prices. For the engineers themselves, it opened up opportunities for their continued professional growth; for some this would even mean the ability to continue to work in the profession—it would also contribute to ending the loss of important human capital in industry.

These human values were important elements in St. Thomas' decision to establish an engineering program. Whatever enhances the quality of life for people is a religious value—one shared by all religions, although not all see it as directly tied to one's work. Whatever helps human beings develop their God-given potential, whatever increases human dignity, is sharing in the work of the Creator and Redeemer. A religious value was present, but perhaps not to the degree found in other programs because of the technical nature of engineering.

In making the decision, the considerable risk involved in an unfamiliar venture, one not even commonly found in schools of engineering, had to be weighed against the human good that could be accomplished and the possibility of establishing an early position in the new field of manufacturing engineering. An important factor in the success of such an undertaking is always leadership. Fortunately there was on the faculty a very capable person who had been championing the cause of a graduate degree in engineering. He understood the kind of university St. Thomas is, its strengths and limitations. And he was completely dedicated to the preservation of manufacturing, especially small, privately-owned enterprises.[1]

The decision was made to start the program at the master's level.

On reflection, the process of consultation and the identification of needs stand out. They both began when the university became aware of a shortage of engineers. As time went on, a great deal was learned about the state of engineering education and about what was a most pressing need. A similar process of consultation had taken place for previous critical decisions, but none was so detailed and lengthy. As it became clear that a new kind of exciting program was being considered, persons volunteered to teach in it: they wanted a part in something that would make a difference and advance their specialty in engineering. The objection that faculty were not available for a program at the cutting edge because the advances were being made in business and not in academia may be valid for full-time faculty but not for adjunct faculty. Many highly

---

[1] On the importance of a champion for a new undertaking, see Thomas J. Peters and Robert H. Waterman, Jr., *In Search of Excellence* (New York: Harper and Row, 1982) esp. ch. 7.

competent, dedicated, and qualified people were available to teach on an adjunct basis alongside a core of proficient full-time faculty. A retired director of research at DuPont travels from Delaware to Minnesota every year to teach a course in polymers. A former 3M vice president teaches manufacturing excellence. A former director of manufacturing at Honeywell teaches classes in automation. A vice president of safety at General Mills teaches a course in industrial safety. A former vice president of 3M is the assistant dean of the program. The list of highly qualified persons goes on.

It was fascinating to participate in this process. It started with nothing more than a desire to be of service. It drew in a great variety of knowledgeable people, some encouraging, some discouraging. First one field of engineering, then another was considered; one type of student, then another. Finally, it was evident what the decision had to be.

The moment of decision, when the uncertainty, the ambiguity, disappears and is replaced by certitude, clarity, confidence, is akin to the moment of creativity in many other fields. There may be a long distance to travel between that moment and the implementation of the decision, but the most difficult, most important and challenging, even if sometimes the most frustrating, moment has been reached. It is a time of both relief and exhilaration, as well as satisfaction.

After the university resolved to establish a master's degree, a request for some financial assistance was presented to the Minnesota legislature. It recognized the need for more engineers and had recently authorized three new programs, but they were not located in the center of the state's population and were not able to accommodate working people. The governor supported the university's proposal in his budget recommendations, and a majority of the appropriations subcommittee of the higher education committee were favorable; however, some educational institutions opposed it, fearful that it might somehow affect the appropriation for student financial aid and other purposes. After a heated discussion, the chairperson of the legislative subcommittee exercised the chair's prerogative and kept the proposal from coming to a vote at the very end of the legislative session. Thus, the state lost an opportunity to contribute to needed education at the very center of the metropolitan area, which contains about one-half of the state's population and most of its manufacturing.

Despite this opposition, St. Thomas moved forward in its efforts to establish its master's degree program in manufacturing engineering. It was an immediate success—evidence of the need. In its first full year of operation 112 students enrolled; in 1990 the program received accreditation from the Accreditation Board for Engineering and Technology (ABET); and by 1994 the number of students had increased to 261.

With the experience thus obtained, the university began to study the establishment of an undergraduate program in engineering, and in the fall of 1993 the undergraduate faculty approved a bachelor of science degree in manufacturing engineering. This recommendation was accepted by the board of trustees to begin in the fall of 1994. The degree was approved by the Minnesota Higher Education Coordinating Board on April 21, 1994. (In the spring of 1998, the university announced the establishment of a bachelor degree in mechanical engineering.) St. Thomas had founded a school of engineering by a process that followed an unusual sequence—a graduate program before an undergraduate program. But more importantly, the university's capacity to serve the community grew.

The school of engineering, with its interest in the application of computer technology to engineering, especially to manufacturing, is a natural ally of education in computer science. St. Thomas began teaching computer courses in the early 1960s, using rented off-campus facilities. It launched its own computer center in 1963 with the gift of a used and somewhat outdated computer. In 1968, it became the first private college in Minnesota to offer an undergraduate degree in computer science. It focused primarily on the design and development of applied software.

From the beginning, students majoring in computer science (called quantitative methods) took not only courses in applied computer science, but also five or six courses in related fields plus the core courses required of all students. The goal was, and is, a broadly educated person as well as one equipped in the computer science area. By the academic year of 1994–95, there were 121 students majoring and approximately 50 students minoring in computer science in addition to a great number taking one or more courses in connection with another field or just for their own knowledge.

At the very start of the inquiry into what the university might do in computer technology, it became clear that perhaps eighty percent of the growth in the computer industry would be in software. To explore the possibilities of a graduate program in the field of computer software, a group was drawn together from the leading companies employing software, such as 3M, Honeywell, IBM, Sperry, Control Data, and NCR Comten. As a result of its deliberations, St. Thomas presented a program for a master of science degree in software to the Minnesota

Higher Education Coordinating Board in December 1984, which gave its approval. The program began in the spring semester of 1985 with fifty-two students.

In seeking approval to grant the master's degree, the university stated in its proposal that the program's purpose was to satisfy the need for graduate education in software engineering "through offering courses in technology, methodology, and management of the design, development, implementation, and maintenance of reliable and cost-effective software systems that meet the requirements of the user." The effort would be to apply theoretical concepts to the situations that the user would encounter in business. This would mean that not only the technical problems would be studied but the legal, ethical, and human concerns as well. The program would also seek to create an awareness of the continuing need for software education in a rapidly changing and highly technological society so that students would become lifelong learners as this dynamic field developed.

When the program began, there were only three other such programs in the country, on the West Coast, on the East Coast, and in the South. None was like the one at St. Thomas, which was both innovative and creative—the others had been designed either to be theoretical or to serve specific businesses. One of the innovative features of the university's program was to substitute for a master's thesis a problem for students to solve, either in their company or another one. It is thought to be the first to make this substitution.

Today there are about fifteen master's programs in software in the United States and several in Europe, but the largest is St. Thomas' with more than five hundred students. Like the engineering program, it employs a number of adjunct professors whose full-time equivalent figure is approximately the same as that of the full-time faculty. They are a great asset, bringing to the students the latest technologies as applied in the most advanced industries. Consequently, they fit the program's purpose very well, namely, educating people to be practicing software professionals, by emphasizing developing and future technologies, to better prepare the students for the workplace in which they will find themselves and to prepare their businesses for global competition.

The courses are offered on the St. Paul and Minneapolis campuses, in the center in Owatonna, and on-site at company locations. In addition to two master's programs there are certificate programs that provide courses but do not require enough credits to qualify for a graduate degree. There are also programs called mini-master certificates which provide in a series of seven or eight evening presentations an overview or summary of the required courses for the master's degree. This gives the people who attend the lectures an indication of what the degree requirements will be if they want to work for it and gives a quick overview of the state of the discipline as well. Finally, there are a number of special noncredit seminars and lectures.

The certificate program of nine courses for credit serves about twelve hundred people a year while about two hundred companies send employees to the degree programs. In the fall of 1994 there were ninety new students registered in degree programs; there were also thirty-five new students in other programs, the largest enrollment of new students in the graduate program's ten-year history. An analysis of these shows that the mean age was thirty-one; twenty-eight percent were women; and the mean years of work experience at the time of entering the program was eight. Over the years the number of courses offered has increased to almost fifty, plus the opportunity for many special arrangements according to the needs of individual students.

An interesting development is a cooperative program with the school of graduate management in which students who are working for a master's in business administration may take certain courses in software and information management.

The programs in software have proven to be closely integrated into the needs of the community, serving businesses, professional organizations, educational institutions, and many other enterprises. Clearly oriented toward practical use, their steady growth is a clear indication that they are fulfilling their purpose. This consistent growth year after year has taken place with almost no advertising, but principally through word of mouth by satisfied students and their employers. The program is a good example of how an educational institution in concert with business and professional people can identify needs and then draw together the human and other resources required to meet them. The result is an increase in the level of education for career people and, consequently, the enhancement of their performance to the benefit of the whole community. From beginning to end, St. Thomas' graduate program in computer science has been an example of our commitment to serve the community.

17

Religion in the Mission of a University

This book emphasizes religious commitment within a university's mission. Religion, as it influences the education of young people, can build better people and better communities. It can energize a university to be of greater service to the community, can become an agent for good in the marketplace and the public square.

Within the university itself religion should not be just a carry-over from an earlier age, a sort of passive or ceremonial presence in its life and relegated to only the private lives of students and staff. On the contrary, it should be a powerful asset, a dynamic force for good. But for it to be so, the university must place it "up front" in its curriculum and daily life. Then it can help its students achieve fuller and more satisfying lives and bring their religious convictions to bear in their public lives. So this book has argued.

What is needed today is a fundamental orientation that applies religious principles to the institutions of American society, and higher education can do much to bring moral values into play in a community. Religion can be an effective agent of change. In a rapidly changing society with ever increasing educational needs, higher education must be willing to step forward and serve the community in new and important ways, including education in values. Failure to do so will result in graduate schools becoming less relevant and our country will be the poorer.

Our society faces problems that seem to be ever more serious and more intractable. Education alone, including that closely related to religion, cannot solve all these, but it can be an important, even necessary, partner in meeting the challenges of today. Creative, energetic, and moral leadership is required in many sectors. Perhaps this small volume has shed some light on addressing societal concerns by sketching out how one university has tried to be a responsive and constructive servant. My hope is that St. Thomas' experience may be of value to educators, to parents of college students, to supporters and friends of education, and to informed citizens.

There are so many ways in which higher education can benefit people and their communities. Certainly a most basic one is to provide excellent education and thereby produce people who are empowered to contribute to the well-being of their fellow citizens, people who not only have skills, but also character and moral commitment to serve. A privatized religion is not enough. Religion must be related to all phases of life and that clearly includes the realm in which one earns a living, whether it be business or some other sphere.

For religion to be related to the community, the university must provide a curriculum that integrates ethics in every discipline insofar as possible. Such an education gives a sense of wholeness to one's life and greater meaning to one's work. This is a large order for higher education today because for too long it has excluded moral principles. The diversity of people's religious beliefs will make it all the more difficult to achieve a degree of common ground. Nonetheless some advancement is possible if there is the will to work at it. Church-related universities should have an easier time in bringing about an integration of values with various academic disciplines. These schools should be leaders and initiators in moving higher education to a more passionate engagement with real life. Although achieving integral education is probably the most difficult task in universities, it is also the most rewarding. But providing a course in religion and even chapel services, as valuable as these are, will not alone bring about the move from privatized religion to public religious discourse and ethical conduct.

While the main thrust of this book has been education for a fuller life, for both private and public life, there are a number of supporting considerations that are related in bringing ethics into higher education. One of these is leadership. A special kind of leadership, namely, entrepreneurial leadership, which is risk-taking, innovative, and willing to seize the moment of opportunity, can move a university in the desired direction. Ultimately leadership comes back to character, integrity, and a track record that gives confidence that the institution will succeed. Entrepreneurial leadership that really moves an institution ahead needs conviction, a conviction so deep that it is part of the life-stance of the leaders.

In an effort to be as specific as possible, this book has concentrated on one university and on only certain aspects of its history. Nevertheless, the ideas and ideals that have been drawn out of that history have broader meaning. Attention has been given to certain developments that are important to higher education and the community: liberal arts, business, institutional culture, communication, technology, environment, and a new metropolitan campus. There are other areas that could have been analyzed, such as seminaries, teacher preparation, social work, counseling, and the list goes on. However, those selected are sufficient to give evidence that the commitment to serve the community can be enlarged and enhanced by a deep-seated commitment to religious values and principles.

The religious character of a university is seldom looked at as an active, dynamic element at its core, playing an essential role in its direction and energy. This study has shown how religious values and commitment to the community, under entrepreneurial leadership, play out in specific academic programs and how they can change and give new energy and outreach to a university and its community.

Bibliography

Adler, Mortimer J. "Labor, Leisure, and Liberal Education" (1951). In *Reforming Education: The Opening of the American Mind.* Ed. Geraldine Van Dorn. New York: Collier Macmillan, 1988.

Birnbaum, Robert. *How Academic Leadership Works.* San Francisco: Jossey-Bass, 1992.

———. *How Colleges Work.* San Francisco: Jossey-Bass, 1988.

Burtchaell, James Tunstead. "The Decline and Fall of the Christian College." *First Things* 12 (March 1991) 16–29; 13 (April 1991) 30–38.

———. *The Dying of the Light.* Grand Rapids, Mich.: Eerdmans, 1998.

Byron, William J., S.J. *Quadrangle Considerations.* Chicago: Loyola University Press, 1989.

Carter, Stephen L. *The Culture of Disbelief: How American Law and Politics Trivialize Religious Devotion.* New York: Basic Books, 1993.

Caux Round Table Principles for Business Conduct. Caux Institute for Corporate Responsibility, Minneapolis. Washington, D.C., 1995.

Chappell, Tom. *The Soul of a Business.* New York: Bantam Books, 1993.

Coles, Robert. *The Call of Service.* New York: Houghton Mifflin Co., 1991.

College and University Newsletter, 3 February 1967. National Catholic Educational Association, Washington, D.C.

Commission on Strengthening Presidential Leadership. *Presidents Make a Difference.* Washington, D.C.: Association of Governing Boards of Universities and Colleges, 1984.

"Confessions of a Public University Refugee." Association of Governing Boards. *Trusteeship* 4 (May–June 1996).

Conger, Jay A. *Learning to Lead.* San Francisco: Jossey-Bass, 1992.

Connors, Joseph B. *Journey Toward Fulfillment.* St. Paul, Minn.: College of St. Thomas, 1986.

Cotter, John P., and James L. Heskett. *Corporate Culture and Performance.* New York: Free Press, 1992.

Covey, Stephen R. *The Seven Habits of Highly Effective People.* New York: Simon & Schuster, 1989.

Current Issues in Catholic Education 14 (summer 1993) 3–4.

Daly, John, S.J., and others. "Coeducational Feasibility Study." 15 January 1976. University of St. Thomas Archives.

Deal, Terrence E., and Allan A. Kennedy. *Corporate Cultures*. Reading, Mass.: Addison-Westley, 1982.

Fisher, James L., and others. *The Effective College President*. New York: MacMillan and American Council on Education, 1988.

Greeley, Andrew. "The Catholic Imagination and the Catholic University." *Current Issues in Catholic Higher Education* 12, no. 1 (summer 1991) 36–40.

Greenleaf, Robert K. *Servant*. Peterborough, N.H.: Windy Row Press, 1988.

Hassel, David J. *City of Wisdom*. Chicago: Loyola University Press, 1983.

Hesburgh, Theodore M. *The Hesburgh Papers*. Kansas City: Andrews & McMeel, 1979.

_____, ed. *The Challenge and Promise of a Catholic University*. South Bend: Notre Dame Press, 1994.

John XXIII, Pope. *Mater et Magistra*. Acta Apostolicae Sedis 53 (1961); [*Mater et Magistra*. Trans. William J. Gibbons. New York: Paulist Press, 1962].

_____. *Pacem in Terris*. Acta Apostolicae Sedis 55 (1963); [*Pacem in Terris*. Washington, D.C.: National Catholic Welfare Conference, 1963].

John Paul II, Pope. *Centesimus Anus* (On the Hundreth Anniversary of *Rerum Novarum*). *Origins* 21 (16 May 1991).

_____. *Apostolic Constitution*. Ex Corde Ecclesiae *of the Supreme Pontiff John Paul II on Catholic Universities*. *Origins* 20 (4 October 1991).

Ker, Ian. *John Henry Newman*. New York: Oxford University Press, 1990.

Langan, John P. *The Catholic University in Church and Society*. Washington: Georgetown University Press, 1993.

Lynch, William F., S.J. *Christ and Apollo: The Dimensions of the Literary Imagination*. New York: Sheed and Ward, 1960.

Manier, Edward, and John W. Houck, eds. *Academic Freedom and the Catholic University*. Notre Dame, Ind.: Fides, 1967.

Maritain, Jacques. *The Education of Man*. Ed. Donald and Idella Gallagher. 1951. Reprint New York: Doubleday, 1962.

Marsden, George M. *The Outrageous Idea of Christian Scholarship*. New York: Oxford University Press, 1997.

_____. *The Soul of the American University: From Protestant Establishment to Established Nonbelief*. New York: Oxford University Press, 1994.

Melady, Thomas Patrick, ed. *Catholics in the Public Square*. Huntington, Ind.: Our Sunday Visitor, 1995.

Minnesota Principles (Minneapolis: Center for Ethical Business Cultures, 1992).

Mintzberg, Henry. "The Manager's Job: Folklore and Fact." *Harvard Business Review* (July–August 1976); (March–April 1990).

National Council of Catholic Bishops. *Catholic Higher Education and the Pastoral Mission of the Church*. *Origins* 10 (13 November 1980).

_____. *The Challenge of Peace: God's Promise and Our Response. Origins* 13 (13 May 1991).

_____. *Economic Justice for All: Catholic Social Teaching and the U.S. Economy. Origins* 16 (27 November 1986) 1ff.

Newman, John Henry. *The Idea of a University.* Reprint. New York: Doubleday & Co., 1959.

_____. *The Scope and Nature of University Education.* Reprint, New York: E. P. Dutton, 1958.

_____. *Sermons Preached on Various Occasions.* London: Longmans, Green, 1894.

O'Brien, David J. *From the Heart of the American Church.* Maryknoll, N.Y.: Orbis Books, 1994.

Paul VI, Pope. Nostra Aetate: *Declaration on the Relationship of the Church to Non-Christian Religions.* In *The Conciliar and Post Conciliar Documents of Vatican II.* Ed. Flannery Austin. Vol 1. New York: Costello, 1992.

Peck, Robert A. "The Entrepreneurial College Presidency." *Educational Journal* (winter, 1983) 18–25.

Pelikan, Jeroslav. *The Idea of the University.* New Haven: Yale University Press, 1992.

_____. *Mary through the Centuries: Her Place in the History of Culture.* New Haven: Yale University Press, 1996.

Peters, Thomas J., and Robert H. Waterman, Jr. *In Search of Excellence.* New York: Harper and Row, 1982.

Reinert, Paul C. *The Urban Catholic University.* New York: Sheed & Ward, 1970.

Schon, Donald A. *The Reflective Practitioner.* New York: Basic Books, 1983.

Sofield, Loughlan, and Donald H. Kuhn. *The Collaborative Leader: Listening to the Wisdom of God's People,* Notre Dame, Ind.: Ave Maria, 1995.

Terry, Robert. "Intuitive Leadership: A Research Project of the Reflective Leadership Center." Hubert H. Humphrey Institute of Public Affairs. Minneapolis: University of Minnesota Press, 1988.

Vatican Council II: *Gravissimum Educationis. Acta Apostolicae Sedis* 58 (28 October 1965); [Gravissimum Educationis: *Declaration on Christian Education.* In *The Basic Sixteen Documents: Constitutions, Decrees, Declarations.* Ed. Austin Flannery. Northport, N.Y.: Costello, 1996)].

_____. *Pastoral Constitution on the Church in the Modern World.* In *The Documents of Vatican II.* Ed. Walter Abbott. New York: New Century, 1966.

Wegener, Charles. *Liberal Education and the Modern University.* Chicago: University of Chicago Press, 1978.

Whitehead, Alfred North. *The Aims of Education.* New York: Free Press, 1967.

Index